The
Chauvinist's
Bedside Book

To Susan de Stein,
who understands

The Chauvinist's Bedside Book

DAVID OLIVE

Illustrated by Barry Blitt

ROBERT HALE • LONDON

Printed in Great Britain by
St Edmundsbury Press, Bury St Edmunds, Suffolk

Contents

	Preface	9
	Acknowledgments	15
1	The Lesser Sex	17
2	The Even Lesser Sex: Prehistoric Man	31
3	Prefeminist Woman	60
4	The Bully Pulpit	78
5	Political Affairs	85
6	Annals of Commerce	112
7	Science & Academe	120
8	Arts & Entertainment	127
9	The Sporting Life	162
10	The Flame of Coexistence	177
	Index to Quoted Subjects	189

Notwithstanding all that wit, or malice, or pride, or prudence will be able to suggest, men and women must at last pass their lives together.

—SAMUEL JOHNSON

Just remember, we're all in this alone.

—LILY TOMLIN

Preface

The wife ought not to have any feelings of her own but join with her husband in his moods.
— PLUTARCH, Greek biographer and moralist

Ivana and I don't have tremendous fights. . . . There's not a lot of disagreement, because ultimately Ivana does exactly as I tell her to do.
— DONALD TRUMP, Queens-born real-estate mogul

When the dust is settled, the spoils distributed, and the writers pen the final history of the war between the sexes, they may well confirm Virginia Woolf's succinct and wry observation that, "The history of men's opposition to women's emancipation is more interesting perhaps than the story of emancipation itself." That opposition has historically covered both word and deed, although deeds are most visible in the foreground today, fueled by such battles as the persecution of Anita Hill in 1991 by an all-male Senate panel, the alleged sexual assault of twenty-six female Navy aviators by their male counterparts during the notorious Tailhook Convention the same year, and the revelations that Senator Bob Packwood made unsolicited sexual advances toward a small army of female associates during his Senate career. But of course historical records are comprised of words, and as the quotations in this collection bear out, the battle is as old as recorded history. And since men have pretty well dominated and controlled recorded history, the battle has been more one-sided than most.

This compilation of outrageous, politically incorrect sayings stretches across the ages from ancient times to modern, revealing a low estimation of women held by men *and* women in every field of endeavor, from politics to religion, commerce to the arts, and sports to popular entertainment.

It is startling, and sobering, to reflect that so many otherwise gifted men and women of vision and achievement—including those engaged in the study of relations between men and women—have failed to see past the centuries-old dogma that holds women to be inferior to men. Aristotle gave us a spiritual understanding of the universe, but he also believed that "the virtues of men are nobler than those of women." The emancipating theologian Martin Luther speculated that "Girls begin to talk and to stand on their feet sooner than boys because weeds always grow up more quickly than good crops." Leo Tolstoy's literary characterizations were informed by a personal conviction that "all disasters, or an enormous proportion of them, are due to the dissoluteness of women," which may help explain author Kaye Gibbons's statement, "I haven't read *War and Peace*, but that's a man's book anyway."

"Direct thought is not an attribute of femininity," the inventive Thomas Edison told the readers of *Good Housekeeping* in 1912. Obsessed with the proper role of women as mothers, Benjamin Spock worried that, "When women are encouraged to be competitive, too many of them become disagreeable," echoing in an only slightly more gentle way Pierre Auguste Renoir's impressions that "women who are authors, lawyers, and politicians are monsters."

History's most famous exponents of liberty have rarely understood their task to include the liberation of women as well as men. "We hold these truths to be self-evident," reads the declaration adopted by the

Continental Congress in Philadelphia (the City of Brotherly Love) on July 4, 1776, "that all Men are created equal. . . ." Nor had the situation improved much nearly two hundred years later. Stating his view that women were not welcome in his mission to tear down the Establishment, youth leader Abbie Hoffman proclaimed: "The only alliance I would make with the Women's Liberation Movement is in bed."

Women often have figured prominently in an unhelpful chorus. Phyllis Schlafly, the anti-feminist activist who has said that, "Feminism is a failed ideology that produces women who are burned-out and bitter," is only the best-known of the backsliders (although sensationalist academic and author Camille Paglia—"If civilization had been left in female hands, we would still be living in grass huts"—is giving her a run for the money). As editor of the mass-market *Cosmopolitan* for more than twenty years, few women are in a position to influence more women than Helen Gurley Brown, who has complained that, "There aren't enough men to go around . . . Every time there's a plane accident, it's one hundred men dead . . . and I literally think, 'Why couldn't some *women* have been on that flight?' "

Some women, although off to a progressive start, have changed midstream. Clare Boothe, journalist, playwright (*The Women*), congresswoman and ambassador, was an accomplished careerist before she met *Time* co-founder Henry Luce. Still, she was convinced that, "A woman's best protection is—the right man." "In passing, I would like to say that the first time Adam had a chance he laid the blame on woman," said Nancy Astor in 1923, getting off to a promising start as the first woman to sit in the British House of Commons. By 1955, Astor was confessing that, "My vigor, vitality and cheek repel me. I am the kind of woman I would run from."

Remember "Hanoi Jane," the actress who defied Lyndon Johnson, the Pentagon, and her staunchly conservative father by taking her anti-war protests to the heart of North Vietnam? By 1991, Jane Fonda, peddler of "Make it *burn*" workout tapes, was devoting her energies to hyperexercise, the kind of appearance-enhancing obsession decried in Naomi Wolf's *The Beauty Myth*: "We do this," Fonda explained, "because we want our guys to find us attractive." In Fonda's case, the guy in question is broadcasting magnate Ted Turner, founder of Cable News Network (CNN) and *Time's* 1991 Man of the Year, who hinted at his looming liaison with Fonda in 1988, saying, "I'm getting a divorce and dating a much younger woman. There's no way I can keep my wife *and* girlfriend happy at the same time."

This book is meant to be read two ways: The main text is a compilation of quotes offering ample evidence that men have emerged from the primordial ooze with a few of their reptilian aspects intact, and that many women are their willing allies in erecting walls against progress toward true equality between the sexes. As a necessary antidote to the crushing ignorance these quotes betray, a selection of enlightened comments appears throughout the text, highlighted with the title "Counterpoint." Locating these signs of intelligent life on the planet Sexual Coexistence has taken up by far the greater part of the labors in assembling this work—a task that has similarly frustrated previous inquirers. In their *New International Dictionary of Quotations* (New American Library, 1986), authors Hugh Rawson and Margaret Miner—after quoting Menander's observation that, "There is nothing worse than a woman—even a good woman!"—excuse themselves from imposing further punishment on the reader, noting that "This [hostility] pretty well sums up the great majority of established quotes on women, most of which we did not feel compelled to include."

My own compulsion to gather this surfeit of quotes from the backwater of primitive thought has been the occasion for moments of deep disappointment and even revulsion, but hard truths must be faced honestly. I hope the reader's spirits, like mine, will be lifted by the wise and witty comments highlighted in the text, and by the signs of progress around us—like that of United States president Bill Clinton breaking with tradition by choosing not to hide from view the strength he draws from his wife. Early in his administration he appointed Hillary Rodham Clinton to head a task force on health-care reform with the straightforward explanation that she is "better at organizing and leading people from a complex beginning to a certain end than anybody I've ever worked with in my life."

In time, the increasingly prominent roles filled by capable women will no longer be regarded in any quarter with astonishment or derision. When the long chapter of misunderstanding and insensitivity between the sexes is closed and words are no longer wielded as weapons, collections such as this may be more celebratory. Even then, it may be the deeds that are most telling. "I hate discussions of feminism that end up with who does the dishes," says one of Marilyn French's characters in *The Women's Room*. "So do I," says her friend. But at the end, there are always the damned dishes.

A great many dishes have been washed since she first wrote those words, increasing numbers of them by men. But one need look no further than the evening news or the pages of this book to see that we still have a long way to go. "You're fooling yourself," Bill Cosby said, "if you think you've got new and improved males because you see three or four dudes out there doing diapers and dishes."

Acknowledgments

I wish to thank the staff of G. P. Putnam's Sons for their assistance in making this book possible; and to acknowledge the generosity of Edwin O'Dacre and *The Globe and Mail* for granting me a leave of absence to complete the work. In particular, I am grateful to my editor, Steve Ross, for his inspiration; and to Joann Webb and Margaret Wente for lessons in life.

• 1 •

The Lesser Sex

There is a good principle which created order, light and man, and an evil principle which created chaos, darkness, and woman.

PYTHAGORAS, *Greek philosopher* (*532?–500? B.C.*)

A woman takes off her claim to respect along with her garments.

HERODOTUS, *Greek historian* (*5th century B.C.*)

Of those who were born as men, all that were cowardly and spent their life in wrongdoing were transformed at the second birth into women. . . . Such is the origin of women and of all that is female.

PLATO, *Greek philosopher* (*about 427–347 B.C.*)

The male is by nature superior, and the female inferior; and the one rules, and the other is ruled; this principle, of necessity, extends to all mankind. . . . The lower sort are by nature slaves, and it is better for them as for all inferiors that they should be under the rule of a master.

ARISTOTLE, *Greek philosopher* (*384–322 B.C.*)

─────────── C O U N T E R P O I N T ───────────

No one can make you feel inferior without your consent.
                                    ELEANOR ROOSEVELT

───────────────── ◆ ─────────────────

The virtues of a naturally higher class are more noble than those of a naturally lower class; thus the virtues of men are nobler than those of women.

ARISTOTLE

Although there may be exceptions to the order of nature, the male is by nature fitter for command than the female, just as the elder and full-grown is superior to the younger and more immature.

ARISTOTLE

The female is, as it were, an impotent male, for it is through a certain incapacity that the female is female, being incapable of concocting the nutriment [menstrual fluid] into semen because of the coldness of her nature.

ARISTOTLE

We should look upon the female state as it were a deformity, though one that occurs in the ordinary course of nature.

ARISTOTLE

─────────── C O U N T E R P O I N T ───────────

*Women—the greatest undeveloped natural resource in
the world today.*

EDWARD STEICHEN

───────────────── ◆ ─────────────────

The male is more courageous than the female, and more sympathetic
in the way of standing by to help. Even in the case of molluscs, when
the cuttlefish is struck with the trident the male stands by to help the
female; but when the male is struck the female runs away.

ARISTOTLE

Mistresses we keep for pleasure, concubines for daily attendance
upon our persons, wives to bear us legitimate children and to be our
faithful housekeepers.

DEMOSTHENES, *Greek orator (385?–322 B.C.)*

─────────── C O U N T E R P O I N T ───────────

*It is funny the two things most men are proudest of is the
thing that any man can do and does in the same way, that is
being drunk and being the father of their son.*

GERTRUDE STEIN

───────────────── ◆ ─────────────────

Revenge, we find,
Ever the pleasure of a petty mind,
And hence so dear to poor weak womanhood.

JUVENAL, *Roman satirist (c. A.D. 60–c. 130)*

Man, but not woman, is made in the image of God. It is plain from this that women should be subject to their husbands, and should be as slaves.

GRATIAN, *12th-century Italian theologian*

Girls begin to talk and to stand on their feet sooner than boys because weeds always grow up more quickly than good crops.

MARTIN LUTHER, *German religious reformer (1483–1546)*

────────────── **COUNTERPOINT** ──────────────

Behind every successful man is a surprised woman.

MARYON PEARSON, wife of Lester Pearson,
prime minister of Canada, 1963–1968

──────────────── ◆ ────────────────

Women are like *Flies*, which feed among us at our Table; or *Fleas* sucking our very blood, who leave not our most retired places free from their familiarity, yet for all their fellowship will they never be tamed nor commanded by us.

JOHN DONNE, *English poet (1573–1631)*

The souls of women are so small
That some believe they have none at all.

SAMUEL BUTLER, *British satirical poet (1612–1680)*

Frailty, thy name is woman!
> WILLIAM SHAKESPEARE, *English poet and dramatist*
> *(1564–1616)*

A woman's counsel brought us first
   to woe,
And made her man his paradise
   forego,
Where at heart's ease he liv'd, and
   might have been
As free from sorrow as he was from
   sin.
> JOHN DRYDEN, *English poet and dramatist (1631–1700)*

———————— **COUNTERPOINT** ————————

I believe in women. Men are just unsubstantiated rumors.
   Canadian author and broadcaster ERIKA RITTER

———————— ◆ ————————

But what is woman? Only one of nature's agreeable blunders.
> ABRAHAM COWLEY, *English poet and essayist (1618–1667)*

It therefore being necessary that the last determination (i.e. the
rule) should be placed somewhere, it naturally falls to the man's share
as the abler and the stronger.
> JOHN LOCKE, *English philosopher (1632–1704)*

─────────────── C O U N T E R P O I N T ───────────────

The true liberation of women cannot take place without the liberation of men. . . . The challenge which we, both men and women, must meet is that of living for a peaceful revolution and not dying for a revolution that would be cruel and, ultimately, illusory.

THERESE CASGRAIN, Quebec feminist, in 1960

──────────────── ◆ ────────────────

Most women have no characters at all.

ALEXANDER POPE, *English poet (1688–1744)*

Men, some to Business, some to Pleasure take;
But every Woman is at heart a Rake.

ALEXANDER POPE

Women will avoid the wicked not because it is unright, but only because it is ugly. . . . Nothing of duty, nothing of compulsion, nothing of obligation! . . . They do something only because it pleases them. . . . I hardly believe that the fair sex is capable of principles.

IMMANUEL KANT, *German philosopher (1724–1804)*

─────────────── C O U N T E R P O I N T ───────────────

Normal men have killed perhaps one hundred million of their fellow normal men in the last fifty years.

Scottish psychiatrist R. D. LAING

──────────────── ◆ ────────────────

Girls should always be submissive, but mothers should not always be inexorable. . . . Indeed I should not be sorry if sometimes she were allowed to exercise a little cunning, not to elude punishment but to escape having to obey. Guile is a natural gift of her sex; and being convinced that all natural dispositions are good and right in themselves, I think that this one should be cultivated like the rest. The characteristic cunning with which women are endowed is an equitable compensation for their lesser strength.

JEAN JACQUES ROUSSEAU, *French philosopher* (*1712–1778*)

COUNTERPOINT

Man forgives woman anything save the wit to outwit him.
MINNA ANTRIM, 19th-century Irish writer

◆

A woman is but an animal, and not an animal of the highest order.
EDMUND BURKE, *English statesman* (*1729–1797*)

Women are, of course, capable of being educated, but their minds
are not really adaptable to the higher sciences, philosophy, or certain
of the creative arts. These demand a faculty for the universal.
Women may have good ideas, good taste, and elegance, but they lack
the talent for the ideal.

> GEORG WILHELM FRIEDRICH HEGEL,
> *German philosopher (1770–1831)*

[**W**oman is] a milk-white lamb that bleats for man's protection.

> JOHN KEATS, *English poet (1795–1821)*

"**T**here you have women," put in M. de Renal, with a coarse laugh.
"There's always something wrong with their machinery."

> STENDHAL (Marie Henri Beyle, French novelist and
> essayist; 1783–1842), *Le Rouge et le Noir* (1831)

No woman ever wrote a really good book.

> WILLIAM LAMB (1779–1848), *British prime minister, to
> Queen Victoria in 1838*

Offend her, and she knows not to forgive;
Oblige her, and she'll hate you while you live.

> ALEXANDER POPE

Woman is the mistress of the art of completely embittering the life of
the person on whom she depends.

> JOHANN WOLFGANG VON GOETHE,
> *German writer and scientist (1749–1832)*

—————————— C O U N T E R P O I N T ——————————

Each woman is being made to feel it is her own cross to bear if she can't be the perfect clone of the male superman and the perfect clone of the feminine mystique.

BETTY FRIEDAN, American writer and feminist, author of *The Feminine Mystique, 1963*

——————————— ◆ ———————————

The woman was not taken
  From Adam's head, we know,
To show she must not rule him—
  'Tis evidently so.
The woman she was taken
  From under Adam's arm,
So she must be protected
  From injuries and harm.

ABRAHAM LINCOLN, *United States president (1809–1865), song composed for a friend's wedding*

Women remain children their whole life long, never seeing anything but what is quite close to them, cleaving to the present moment, taking appearance for reality, and preferring trifles to matters of the first importance.

ARTHUR SCHOPENHAUER, *German philosopher (1788–1860)*

That woman is by nature meant to obey may be seen by the fact that every woman who is placed in the unnatural position of complete independence immediately attaches herself to some man by whom she allows herself to be guided and ruled. It is because she needs a lord and master. If she is young, it will be a lover; if she is old, a priest.

ARTHUR SCHOPENHAUER

God made the woman for the use of man, and for the good and increase of the world.

ALFRED LORD TENNYSON, *English poet* (1809–1892)

How did woman first become subject to man as she now is all over the world? By her nature, her sex, just as the negro is and always will be, to the end of time, inferior to the white race, and, therefore, doomed to subjection; but happier than she would be in any other condition, just because it is the law of her nature. The women themselves would not have this law reversed.

editorial in the New York Herald, *1852*

———————— **C O U N T E R P O I N T** ————————

Women who seek to be equal with men lack ambition.
sixties psychedelic prophet TIMOTHY LEARY

———————— ◆ ————————

Woman is nature, hence detestable.

CHARLES PIERRE BAUDELAIRE, *French poet and critic*
(1821–1867)

Woman must obey to find depth to her surface. Surface is woman's nature, foam tossed to and fro on shallow water.

But deep is man's nature; his current flows in subterranean caverns: woman senses his power, but understands it not.

FRIEDRICH NIETZSCHE, *German philosopher and poet*
(*1844–1900*)

Did any woman ever acknowledge profundity in another woman's mind, or justice in another woman's heart?

FRIEDRICH NIETZSCHE

——————— C O U N T E R P O I N T ———————

As long as you know that most men are like children you know everything.

COCO CHANEL, French fashion designer
(1883–1971)

————————— ◆ —————————

Man is more courageous, pugnacious and energetic than woman, and has a more inventive genius. His brain is absolutely larger, but whether or not proportionately to his larger body, has not, I believe, been fully ascertained.

CHARLES DARWIN

Wicked women bother one. Good women bore one. That is the only difference between them.

OSCAR WILDE, *Irish poet and prose writer* (*1854–1900*)

Women, then, are only children of a larger growth; they have an entertaining tattle, and sometimes wit; but for solid reasoning, good sense, I never knew in my life one that had it, or who reasoned or acted consequently to four and twenty hours together.

LORD CHESTERFIELD *(Philip Dormer Stanhope) English statesman and writer (1694–1773), advice to his son*

God created woman. And boredom did indeed cease from that moment—but many other things ceased as well. Woman was God's second mistake.

FRIEDRICH NIETZSCHE

———————— C O U N T E R P O I N T ————————

She did observe, with some dismay, that, far from conquering all, love lazily sidestepped practical problems.
JEAN STAFFORD, American writer (1915–1979)

——————————— ◆ ———————————

In revenge and in love woman is more barbarous than man.

FRIEDRICH NIETZSCHE

So-called decent women differ from whores mainly in that whores are less dishonest.

LEO TOLSTOY, *Russian novelist (1828–1910), in* The Kreutzer Sonata, *1889*

An animal usually living in the vicinity of man and having a rudimentary susceptibility to domestication . . . the woman is lithe and graceful in its movements, is omnivorous and can be taught not to talk.

AMBROSE BIERCE, *American journalist* (*1842?–1914*)

There are only three things in the world that women do not understand: and they are Liberty, Equality and Fraternity.

G. K. CHESTERTON, *English author* (*1874–1936*)

───────────── **C O U N T E R P O I N T** ─────────────

It may be the cock that crows, but it is the hen that lays the eggs.

MARGARET THATCHER, former
British prime minister

───────────── ◆ ─────────────

The female body, even at its best, is very defective in form; it has harsh curves and very clumsily distributed masses; compared to it the average milk-jug, or even cuspidor, is a thing of intelligent and gratifying design.

H. L. MENCKEN, *American journalist* (*1880–1956*)

No one can evade the fact, that in taking up a masculine calling, studying and working in a man's way, woman is doing something not wholly in agreement with, if not directly injurious to, her feminine nature.

CARL JUNG, *Swiss psychologist* (*1875–1961*)

——————— C O U N T E R P O I N T ———————

[If men could menstruate] sanitary supplies would be federally funded and free. Of course, some men would still pay for the prestige of such commercial brands as Paul Newman Tampons, Muhammad Ali's Rope-a-Dope Pads, John Wayne Maxi Pads, and Joe Namath Jock Shields—"For Those Light Bachelor Days."

U.S. author and feminist GLORIA STEINEM

———————— ◆ ————————

From the beginning of time, the female cycle has defined and confined women's role.

a 1960 article in Newsweek *asserts the unalterable debilitating effect of menstruation on aspiring career women*

The truth is that women's income, on average, will always be a fraction of men's, so long as America remains free.

PATRICK BUCHANAN, *American journalist, in 1984*

——————— C O U N T E R P O I N T ———————

Women want mediocre men, and men are working hard to be as mediocre as possible.

MARGARET MEAD, American anthropologist, in 1958

———————— ◆ ————————

·2·

The Even Lesser Sex:
Prehistoric Man

Nothing is more intolerable than a wealthy woman.

JUVENAL (c. A.D. 60–c. 130)

A woman is always buying something.

OVID, *Roman poet* (43 B.C.–A.D. 17?)

Don't you think that robbing a corpse is indicative of a mean, petty and womanish spirit?

SOCRATES *in* Plato's Republic, c. 380 B.C.

When the candles are out all women are fair.

PLUTARCH, *Greek essayist* (c. 46–120 A.D.)

The wife ought not to have any feelings of her own but join with her husband in his moods whether serious, playful, thoughtful, or joking.

PLUTARCH

Should a man in private be without control or guidance in his pleasures and commit some indiscretion with a prostitute or servant girl, the wife should not take it hard or be angry, reasoning that because of his respect for her, he does not include her in his drunken parties, excesses, and wantonness with other women.

PLUTARCH

If you let your wife stand on your toe tonight, she'll stand on your face first thing tomorrow morning.

SIR THOMAS MORE, *English statesman and writer* (1478–1535)

Two women plac'd together makes cold weather.

WILLIAM SHAKESPEARE *in* Henry VIII

─────────── **COUNTERPOINT** ───────────

If you want a thing well done, get a couple of old broads to do it.

actress BETTE DAVIS, first woman president of the Academy of Motion Picture Arts and Sciences, in 1941

───────────── ◆ ─────────────

Win her with gifts, if she respects not words;
Dumb jewels often in their silent kind
More than quick words do move a woman's mind.

WILLIAM SHAKESPEARE *in* Two Gentlemen of Verona

The husband hath by law power and dominion over his wife, and may keep her by force, within the bounds of duty, and may beat her, but not in a violent or cruel manner.

FRANCIS BACON *English philosopher and writer* (1561–1626)

God is thy law, thou mine: to know no more
Is woman's happiest knowledge and her praise.

Eve, to Adam, in JOHN MILTON's Paradise Lost, *1665*

Madam, we took you in order to have children, not to get advice.

CHARLES XI, *King of Sweden from 1660 to 1697, to his wife in response to her pleas on behalf of the petitions of one of his subjects*

It is the male that gives charms to womankind, that produces an air in their faces, a grace in their motions, a softness in their voices, and a delicacy in their complexions.

JOSEPH ADDISON, *English essayist and statesman* (1672–1719)

Keep your eyes wide open before marriage, half shut afterwards.

BENJAMIN FRANKLIN, *American writer, statesman and inventor* (1706–1790)

A perfect woman, nobly planned,
To warn, to comfort, and command.

WILLIAM WORDSWORTH, *English poet* (1770–1850)

Sir, a woman preaching is like a dog walking on his hind legs. It is not done well: but you are surprised to find it done at all.

SAMUEL JOHNSON, *English lexicographer, critic, and essayist (1709–1784)*

Women who are either indisputably beautiful, or indisputably ugly, are best flattered upon the score of their understandings; but those who are in a state of mediocrity are best flattered upon their beauty, or at least their graces; for every woman who is not absolutely ugly thinks herself handsome.

LORD CHESTERFIELD (1694–1773), *advice to his son*

The first and most important quality of a woman is sweetness. . . . She must learn to submit uncomplainingly to unjust treatment and marital wrongs.

JEAN JACQUES ROUSSEAU

Man should be trained for war and woman for the recreation of the warrior.

FRIEDRICH NIETZSCHE

Women have, or ought to have, but little liberty; they are apt to indulge themselves excessively in what is allowed them.

JEAN JACQUES ROUSSEAU

A woman who has a head full of Greek . . . or carries on fundamental controversies about mechanics, might as well have a beard.

IMMANUEL KANT

COUNTERPOINT

Getting along with men isn't what's truly important. The vital knowledge is how to get along with a man, one man.

PHYLLIS McGINLEY, poet and author
(1905–1978)

◆

The husband ought to be able to superintend his wife's conduct, because it is of importance for him to be assured that the children, whom he is obliged to acknowledge and maintain, belong to no one but himself.

JEAN JACQUES ROUSSEAU

A man of sense only trifles with [women], plays with them, humours and flatters them, as he does with a sprightly forward child; but he neither consults them about, nor trusts them with serious matters; though he often makes them believe that he does both; which is the thing in the world that they are proud of; for they love mightily to be dabbling in business (which, by the way, they always spoil); and being justly distrustful, that men in general look upon them in a trifling light, they almost adore that man who talks more seriously to them, and who seems to consult and trust them; I say, who seems; for weak men really do, but wise men only seem to do it.

LORD CHESTERFIELD, *advice to his son*

A sweetheart is a bottle of wine; a wife is a wine bottle.

CHARLES BAUDELAIRE

―――――――― COUNTERPOINT ――――――――

Plain women know more about men than beautiful ones do.
actress KATHARINE HEPBURN

――――――――――― ◆ ―――――――――――

Women, when they have made a sheep of a man, always tell him that he is a lion with a will of iron.

HONORÉ DE BALZAC, *French novelist* (1799–1850)

Between a woman's "yes" and "no" I would not venture to stick a pin.

MIGUEL DE CERVANTES SAAVEDRA, *Spanish novelist* (1547–1616)

I will not say that women have no character; rather, they have a new one every day.

HEINRICH HEINE, *German poet and essayist* (1797–1856)

Nature intended women to be our slaves. . . . They are our property, we are not theirs. . . . They belong to us, just as a tree which bears fruit belongs to the gardener. What a mad idea to demand equality for women! . . . Women are nothing but machines for producing children.

NAPOLÉON BONAPARTE, *French emperor* (1769–1821)

[**W**omen are] sweetly smiling angels with pensive looks, innocent faces, and cash-boxes for hearts.

HONORÉ DE BALZAC

Man is the hunter; woman is his game:
The sleek and shining creatures of the chase,
We hunt them for the beauty of their skins;
They love us for it, and we ride them down.

ALFRED, LORD TENNYSON

For the female of the species is more deadly than the male.
                    RUDYARD KIPLING, *English writer* (*1865–1936*)

The brain-women never interest us like the heart-women; white roses please less than red.
        OLIVER WENDELL HOLMES, *American man of letters* (*1809–1894*)

A woman needs to be taken, not adored.
                            FREDERICK PHILIP GROVE, *German-born Canadian*
                            novelist, in Settlers of the Marsh, *1925*

You are not permitted to kill a woman who has injured you, but nothing forbids you to reflect that she is growing older every minute.
                                            AMBROSE BIERCE

—————————— **C O U N T E R P O I N T** ——————————

I think women are extremely beautiful at forty. . . . I think it's time we started seeing role models of women when they are women and not children.
                        American fashion designer CALVIN KLEIN, in
                        1992, launching an ad campaign featuring
                        40-year-old model Lisa Taylor

——————————— ◆ ———————————

She wore far too much rouge last night and not quite enough clothes; that is always a sign of despair in a woman.
                                            OSCAR WILDE

Don't give a woman advice: one should never give a woman anything she can't wear in the evening.

OSCAR WILDE

Like all young men, you greatly exaggerate the difference between one young woman and another.

GEORGE BERNARD SHAW, *British dramatist* (*1856–1950*), in Major Barbara . . . (*1905*)

──────── C O U N T E R P O I N T ────────

Men's minds are raised to the level of the women with whom they associate.

ALEXANDRE DUMAS, French novelist, in 1830

──────── ◆ ────────

If a man understands one woman he should let it go at that.

ROBERT CHAMBERS (BOB) EDWARDS, *Canadian writer and newspaper publisher* (*1864–1922*)

It hurts me to confess it, but I'd have given ten conversations with Einstein for a first meeting with a pretty chorus girl.

ALBERT CAMUS, *French novelist and dramatist* (*1913–1960*)

A girl whose cheeks are covered with paint
Has an advantage with me over one whose ain't.

OGDEN NASH, *American humorist* (*1902–1971*)

The way to fight a woman is with your hat. Grab it and run.
                    JOHN BARRYMORE, *American actor* (1882–1942)

I didn't say a word. I went over and hit her. I certainly must have knocked a lot of teeth out of her. She ended up in a corner all in a heap.
                    FRANK CAPRA, *Hollywood director* (It's a Wonderful Life),
                                        on his first wife

The husband who wants a happy marriage should learn to keep his mouth shut and his checkbook open.
                    GROUCHO MARX, *American humorist* (1890–1977)

We'll lead an ideal life if you'll just avoid doing one thing: don't think.
                    RONALD REAGAN, *American actor and U.S. President*

I think a man can have two, maybe three affairs while he is married. But three is the absolute maximum. After that, you are cheating.
                    YVES MONTAND, *Italian-born actor*

─────────── **COUNTERPOINT** ───────────

Show me a woman who doesn't feel guilty and I'll show you a man.

                    ERICA JONG, American writer and feminist

────────────── ◆ ──────────────

Here they are—Jayne Mansfield!
> *introduction written for talk-show host Jack Paar by* DICK CAVETT

Buy old masters. They fetch a much better price than old mistresses.
> LORD BEAVERBROOK (MAX AITKEN), *Canadian-born*
> *British press lord* (*1879–1964*)

Nobody works as hard for his money as the man who marries it.
> *American humorist* KIN HUBBARD

A husband should not insult his wife publicly, at parties. He should insult her in the privacy of the home.
> JAMES THURBER, *American humorist and cartoonist* (*1894–1961*)

Never tell. Not if you love your wife. . . . In fact, if your old lady walks in on you, deny it. Yeah. Just flat out and she'll believe it: "I'm tellin' ya. This chick came downstairs with a sign around her neck 'Lay on top of me or I'll die.' I didn't know what I was gonna do . . ."
> LENNY BRUCE, *American comedian* (*1926–1966*)

The only position for women in the Revolution is prone.
> *Afro-American rights activist* STOKELY CARMICHAEL *in 1969*

The only alliance I would make with the Women's Liberation Movement is in bed.
> *U.S. peace activist* ABBIE HOFFMAN *in 1972*

Women are here to serve men. Look at them, they got to squat to piss. Hell, that proves it.

> LARRY FLYNT, *founding publisher of* Hustler *magazine, in 1976*

Live large, stay hard.
> *motto of author* DON PENDLETON'*s paperback fiction hero Mack Bolan*

C O U N T E R P O I N T

Girls had it better from the beginning. Boys can run around fighting wars for made-up reasons with toy guns going kksshh-kksshhh and arguing about who was dead, while girls play in the house with their dolls, creating complex family groups and solving problems through negotiation and role-playing. Which gender is better equipped, on the whole, to live an adult life, would you guess?

> GARRISON KEILLOR in *The New York Times,* 1992

◆

When you run a picture of a nice, clean-cut, all-American girl like this, *get her tits above the fold.*

> ALLEN NEUHARTH, *CEO of Gannett Co., admonishing his editors at* USA Today *in the mid-1980s*

How do you say, "We'd like to drink your bathwater" in Portugese?

> Esquire *magazine in 1988, on actress Sonia Braga, featured in a "Women We Love" article*

Henry VIII . . . didn't get divorced, he just had [his wives'] heads chopped off when he got tired of them. That's a good way to get rid of a woman—no alimony.

TED TURNER, *American broadcasting magnate, in 1983*

Stay away from girls who cry a lot or who look like they get pregnant easily or have careers.

P. J. O'ROURKE, *American satirist and author*

And ladies, he isn't married.

> *NBC anchor* TOM BROKAW *in 1988, telling viewers that John F. Kennedy, Jr., is about to address the Democratic National Convention*

Every married guy cheats on his wife. What's the big deal?

> DON SOFFER, *owner of the yacht* Monkey Business, *on the Gary Hart/Donna Rice affair, in 1988. A photo of Hart and Rice on the yacht was widely published in 1988.*

――――――――― C O U N T E R P O I N T ―――――――――

I've been a man many times. That's what I'm trying to atone for now.

> singer HELEN REDDY in 1991 on her belief in reincarnation

―――――――――――――― ◆ ――――――――――――――

I'm getting a divorce and dating a much younger woman. There's no way I can keep my wife *and* girlfriend happy at the same time.

> TED TURNER *in 1988*

Slap her once or twice, but do not punch her.

> *British judge* CHARLES GARRAWAY *disciplining a man accused of assaulting his girlfriend, in 1988*

What's this about women not having children? It's their only function. Nature demands of them that they be mothers twelve times a year.

YVON LEFEBVRE, *treasurer of the Calgary Coalition for Life, in 1988*

——————————— C O U N T E R P O I N T ———————————

At work, you think of the children you have left at home. At home, you think of the work you've left unfinished. Such a struggle is unleashed within yourself. Your heart is rent.
GOLDA MEIR (1898–1978), former
Israeli prime minister

——————————— ◆ ———————————

Your greatest achievement is to love me.
alleged 1989 telephone conversation in which Britain's
PRINCE CHARLES *responds to longtime friend Camilla Parker-Bowles' assertion that she has never achieved anything*

——————————— C O U N T E R P O I N T ———————————

A woman without a man is like a fish without a bicycle.
GLORIA STEINEM

——————————— ◆ ———————————

A beautiful woman with a brain is like a beautiful woman with a club foot.

fugitive financier BERNARD CORNFELD

I love journalists. If I were a woman, I'd be pregnant all the time because I'd never be able to turn one down.

> *press baron* ROBERT MAXWELL *in 1989*

He isn't a masher . . . this is very harmless. He's a very decent sort of guy.

> *attorney* ROBERT MESHEL *in 1989, defending client Leo Kazan, who allegedly made almost 13,000 obscene telephone calls to women*

She asked for it. The way she was dressed with that skirt you could see everything she had. She was advertising for sex.

> *Juror* ROY DIAMOND *in 1989, explaining why his Ft. Lauderdale, Florida, jury acquitted a man of the rape of a 22-year-old woman who wore a lace skirt, a tank top, and no underpants during the alleged assault*

If the men want to take off their jackets, feel free to. And, if the girls want to take off their blouses, it's all right with me.

> TED TURNER, *addressing the National Press Club in 1989*

Treat him like the king he is.

> ANTHONY C. RENFRO, *author of* A Guide for a Single Woman, *in 1989, on how to treat boyfriends*

Radical feminism, of course, has vowed to destroy the traditional family unit, hates motherhood, hates children for the most part, and promotes lesbian activity.

> *anti-abortion activist* RANDALL TERRY *in the late 1980s*

───────────── C O U N T E R P O I N T ─────────────

If men could get pregnant, abortion would be a sacrament.
Canadian feminist leader LAURA SABIA

───────────────── ◆ ─────────────────

A woman just can't do as much work as a man. I believe that.
REUBEN DAVIS, *commissioner of Jefferson County,*
Alabama, in 1989

Police work is a tough field for women to go into; therefore, we make it tougher for them to complete the course.
Massachusetts state police captain CHARLES APPLETON, *in 1989*

I don't ordinarily allow anyone to use that "Ms." in this courtroom. What if I call you "sweetie"?
federal judge HUBERT TEITELBAUM *to Pittsburgh attorney*
Barbara Wolvovitz, in 1989

Sarah doesn't talk about needing her space and all that other garbage. She works seven days a week and still has time to make me dinner.
actor JAMES WOODS *in 1989, on his fiancée Sarah Owen*

Pageants should be understood within the context of celebrations, as cultural harvests. We're saying, "This is the best of the young womanhood . . . the best of this year's harvest."
U.S. beauty-pageant judge MICHAEL MARSDEN, *in 1989*

It's rare to find a woman with very good mental agility.

> EARL OF SPENCER, *father of Princess Diana, in 1989*

I don't support wife beating but I understand it.

> *late comedian* SAM KINISON, *in 1989*

There's no excuse for any woman out there not to be beautiful with all the soaps and cosmetics around. They should be beautiful so we can look at them, even if they're a dog when they go home at night.

> WALTER JAMES, *cofounder of lingerie maker UndercoverWear Inc., in 1989*

Femininity is goodness, tact, and weakness. Weakness and emotionality should be part of women—otherwise who are we, the rational and strong, going to defend?

> *cosmonaut* GEORGY GRECHKO *in 1989*

———————— C O U N T E R P O I N T ————————

I figure in his next life he'll come back as a slug and someone will put salt on him and that will be the end of him.

> DORIS KINDER of Annandale, Virginia, in 1992, on Donald Trump, while attending a book-signing by Ivana Trump

◆

To manufacture only small sizes is a favor for humanity. I prevent ugly girls from showing off their bad figures.

designer ELIO FIORUCCI *in 1989*

[**I**vana and I] don't have tremendous fights. . . . There's not a lot of disagreement, because ultimately Ivana does exactly as I tell her to do.

real estate mogul DONALD TRUMP *in 1989,*
on his relationship with then-wife Ivana

Don't give me male administrators. They turn on you. But women unhappy at home—in their forties and fifties, after menopause, when they're more consistent—can give untiringly to me of their services.

JOE CLARK, *New Jersey high school principal, in 1989*

I'm looking for a woman with an intense sexual appetite, because I don't ever want to have to cheat.

actor DAVID KEITH *on what he wants in a woman, in 1989*

Women's logic is one of those contradictory terms like military intelligence.

CNN meteorologist FLIP SPICELAND *in 1990*

There's nothing tougher than remembering why you've chased a dame once you've had her.

actor CLINT EASTWOOD *in 1990*

Never be unfaithful to a lover, except with your wife.

P. J. O'ROURKE

Will you still love me when I don't have any money?

DONALD TRUMP *in 1990, attempting a reconciliation with Ivana, who responded, "Yes. I already* did *love you when you didn't have any money, remember?"*

Roses are Red
Orchids R Black
I like my date
When she's on her back.

> *graffiti sprayed on the front of the Sigma Chi frat house at the*
> *University of Texas by its members in 1990*

Their mischief with wives of juniors was seen as a perk of high service.

> *retired Indian general* PREM KUKRETY *in 1990, complaining about*
> *the forced early retirement of four Indian Army generals suspected*
> *of "stealing the affections of a brother officer's wife"*

Rules are like women. They are meant to be violated.

> *Quebec court justice* DENYS DIONNE *in 1990*

COUNTERPOINT

How many men does it take to tile a floor? That depends on
how thin you slice them.

> feminist joke, circa 1986

◆

It's not like she was tortured or chopped up.

> *Manhattan Supreme Court justice* JEROME MARKS *in 1990,*
> *on giving a light sentence to a rape victim's attacker*

I bet that women who keep their own names are less apt to keep their husbands.

TV commentator ANDY ROONEY *in 1990*

Would you like to remind me, too?

Supreme Court justice SANDRA DAY O'CONNOR *in 1991*
after an attorney said in court, "I would like to remind you
gentlemen" of a legal point

Just "Justices" would be fine.

Supreme Court justice BYRON WHITE, *after the same attorney*
later addressed the court, "Justice O'Connor and gentlemen"

As a guy, you're raised to get as much as you can.

actor WOODY HARRELSON, *who played the bartender in the*
TV series Cheers, *on why he has been promiscuous*

Date rape, I assure you, lies in our medium-term future.

P. JAY FETNER, *a member of Yale University's Skull and Bones*
fraternity, in 1991 on why women should be barred from joining

It's like rough sex. You've got to know when to hold back.

New York Post *editor* JERRY NACHMAN *in 1991*
on tabloid journalism

Ninety percent of them are whiners and whimperers. If my wife should ever go on television . . . I would divorce her.

> *U.S. Air Force Major General* BILLY G. McCOY *in 1991, on military wives who talked with reporters about their husbands fighting in the Persian Gulf war*

Go-go dancers, topless dancers, or hookers.

> *characterization of female U.S. Navy pilots by a Navy admiral after the 1991 assault of 26 women by Navy and Marine Corps officers at the annual Tailhook Convention of Navy aviators in Las Vegas*

———————— C O U N T E R P O I N T ————————

If a woman chooses to look sexy, that is her right. If a man chooses to misinterpret her signal, that's his problem.

> SUZY MENKES, American fashion designer, in 1992

————————— ◆ —————————

You know, it really doesn't matter what [the media] write as long as you've got a young and beautiful piece of ass.

> DONALD TRUMP *in 1991*

Feminism was established to allow unattractive women access to mainstream society.

> *talk-show host* RUSH LIMBAUGH *in 1991*

I don't screw around. If I'd done one-third of what people say I have, if I'd had half the women, I'd be a *great* man. But I haven't. I wish I had.

CBS anchor DAN RATHER *in 1991*

There has been no exclusion. We have simply excluded all the women.

NICOLAS ROMANOFF, 69, *a descendant of the last Russian czar, on why there were no female relatives at a 1992 meeting to form a family foundation to help democracy in Russia*

You say, "Good morning," and she wants to make love. You say, "Good afternoon," and she wants to make love. You say, "Good night," and she wants to make love.

actor DON JOHNSON *in 1992, on the sex drive of wife Melanie Griffith*

A similar thing happens when a good-looking scantily attired female walks in. Some of the males' energy fields are disturbed. . . . Magnetic objects buried in the earth respond in similar states of excitement.

an Army Corps of Engineers document, c. 1992, describing a hazardous waste site's "remanent magnetism"

There are pressures on this battlefront that a woman is just not necessarily set up to be able to completely handle and take. We are patriarchal. We believe that men are supposed to lead and that a man's greatest role in our society is to protect a woman.

> *anti-abortion activist* BRYAN BROWN *of the Wichita Rescue Movement in 1992, on the dearth of women leaders in the pro-life movement*

All these femi-Nazis out there, demanding their right to abortion as the most important thing in their life, never ever have to worry about having one anyway. Because who'd want to have sex with 'em?

> RUSH LIMBAUGH *on his WABC (New York) talk radio program in 1992. Comedian Joy Behar, who also has a program on WABC, responded by creating a list of "the top ten reasons why Rush Limbaugh can't get laid," including "Because Lassie said no. . . . It's hard to oink sweet nothings in a woman's ear. . . . Most women do not consider going to a book burning a fun date," and "He can't find a condom big enough to fit over his ego."*

My dream is to save them from nature.

> *fashion designer* CHRISTIAN DIOR, *describing his mission on behalf of women*

They say there's discrimination, so they revoke laws banning women from being truckers, construction workers or miners. . . . Who wants to go home to a wife who smells of cement and has big muscles? [My wife] pilots the stove rather than a truck. That's more appropriate.

> LUIZ CARLOS JACARE LADEIRA, *founding member of the Brazilian Macho Movement, in 1992*

[The fight for the Equal Rights Amendment in Iowa] is about a socialist, anti-family political movement that encourages women to leave their husbands, kill their children, practice witchcraft, destroy capitalism, and become lesbians.

PAT ROBERTSON, *American televangelist and politician, in 1992*

[U.S. Congresswoman] Pat Schroeder doesn't understand the military any more than she understands families, and her recent blathering about so-called sexual harassment in the military proves it. Upset that men will be men, she would [rather] change them to wimps. At the 1991 Tailhook convention, Navy pilots got drunk and pawed females, some in uniform, who were voluntarily in their midst. So what?

A. MAT WERNER, *captain, U.S. Air Force Reserve, in 1992*

──────────── **COUNTERPOINT** ────────────

Dear Dr. Sooth:
This gal I've been dating seems perfect in every way except one—or should I say two. She's an "A" cup, and frankly, I only bed "C"s. How do I broach the subject of implants?
Letter-Perfect

Dear Alphabet Soup for Brains:
Actually, your gal's got an even more pressing problem than implants. She needs to get her head examined to figure out why she's hanging around with a turkey such as yourself. Invest in a blow-up doll: It'll be cheaper and safer for her, and all the same to you.

"DR. SOOTH" column, GQ magazine,
December 1992

──────────── ◆ ────────────

It's harder to be sympathetic to the woman on welfare being interviewed on television when she's fat.

ANDY ROONEY *in 1992*

———————— C O U N T E R P O I N T ————————

I owe every woman in America an apology.
Hustler publisher LARRY FLYNT

———————————— ◆ ————————————

[Gloria Steinem] and her feminist colleagues have labored to break up the family. . . . So to divorcées and to the millions of American children brought up in broken homes and amok in social pathologies, Miss Steinem can present herself as a liberator.

R. EMMETT TYRRELL, JR., *American columnist, in 1992*

Suppose a woman is not legally married but lives with a man. Would you say she is ineligible?

university professor KEIKO HIGUCHI, *on the 1992 Miss Universe preliminary in Japan, when judges disqualified the winner after finding out that she had been married and divorced*

I am convinced . . . that [women] really want, underneath it all, for [the man] to be the decision maker. . . . Wives ought to be subject to their husbands in *everything*. That includes physical relationships.

ROBERT VERNON, *assistant chief of the Los Angeles Police Department, in 1992*

Behind every feminist is either a ruined husband or a ruined father. Feminism is at its core dysfunctional.

RANDALL TERRY, *founder of anti-abortion group Operation Rescue, in 1992*

Will had to reluctantly admit that was true, which has certainly helped him with dates since then.

> *attorney* ROY BLACK *in 1992, on William Kennedy Smith's claim of having sex twice in 30 minutes with Patricia Bowman, who accused him of date rape*

──────────────── C O U N T E R P O I N T ────────────────

Man isn't a noble savage, he's an ignoble savage.
> STANLEY KUBRICK, American filmmaker

──────────────── ◆ ────────────────

·3·

Prefeminist Woman

The Queen is most anxious to enlist everyone who can speak or write to join in checking this mad, wicked folly of "Women's Rights," with all its attendant horrors on which her poor feeble sex is bent, forgetting every sense of womanly feeling and propriety. Woman would become the most hateful, heartless and disgusting of human beings were she allowed to unsex herself; and where would be the protection which man was intended to give the weaker sex?

QUEEN VICTORIA *in the late 19th century*

A woman, if she has the misfortune of knowing anything, should conceal it as well as she can.

JANE AUSTEN, *English novelist (1775–1817)*

I should like to know what is the proper function of women, if it is not to make reasons for husbands to stay at home, and still stronger reasons for bachelors to go out.

GEORGE ELIOT *in* The Mill on the Floss

Gentlemen prefer blondes.
> *American author* ANITA LOOS *in 1925. The financier
> Andrew Mellon responded that, "Gentlemen prefer bonds."*

It isn't that gentlemen really prefer blondes, it's just that we look dumber.
> ANITA LOOS

──────────────── **C O U N T E R P O I N T** ────────────────

It is possible that blondes also prefer gentlemen.
> MAMIE VAN DOREN, American singer

──────────────────── ◆ ────────────────────

A man in the house is worth two in the street.
> *actress* MAE WEST (*1892–1980*)

From birth to age eighteen a girl needs good parents. From eighteen to thirty-five she needs good looks. From thirty-five to fifty-five she needs a good personality. From fifty-five on, she needs good cash.
> SOPHIE TUCKER, *American singer* (*1884–1966*)

You can never be too thin or too rich.
> *American socialite* WALLIS WARFIELD SIMPSON, *who
> married the Duke of Windsor, the former King Edward VIII, in 1937*

─────────── C O U N T E R P O I N T ───────────

She is a water bug on the surface of life.
>GLORIA STEINEM in 1992 on writer Sally
>Quinn, who wrote that feminism is perceived
>as a fringe movement "with overtones of
>lesbianism and man-hating"

───────────────── ◆ ─────────────────

A woman's best protection is—the right man.
>*American playwright, ambassador and congresswoman*
>CLARE BOOTHE LUCE

I live by a man's code, designed to fit a man's world, yet at the same time I never forget that a woman's first job is to choose the right shade of lipstick.
>*actress* CAROLE LOMBARD (*1908–1942*)

─────────── C O U N T E R P O I N T ───────────

When a woman ceases to alter the fashion of her hair, you
guess that she has passed the crisis of her experience.
>MARY HUNTER AUSTIN, suffragist, in 1903

───────────────── ◆ ─────────────────

My vigor, vitality and cheek repel me. I am the kind of woman I would run from.
>NANCY ASTOR, *British parliamentarian*

I require only three things of a man. He must be handsome, ruthless and stupid.

DOROTHY PARKER, *American writer* (*1893–1967*)

A successful man makes more money than his wife can spend. A successful woman is one who can find such a man.

actress LANA TURNER

Kissing your hand may make you feel very, very good, but a diamond and sapphire bracelet lasts forever.

ANITA LOOS

Where's the man could ease a heart
Like a satin gown?

DOROTHY PARKER

An ounce of sequins can be worth a pound of home cooking.

MARILYN VOS SAVANT

I never hated a man enough to give him his diamonds back.

actress ZSA ZSA GABOR

Must a girl always be protected by a man? Not this girl! When I lived in California I sometimes picked a man up in *my* car for a date if his was in the garage, loaned to a friend or—my car was in better shape! (No, he wasn't emasculated and we stayed friends.) Last week at J.F.K. I carried one of *Stephen's* bags. He was loaded with golf clubs and I only had a garment bag and a Vuitton. (No, I *didn't* throw my back out and Stephen and I are still together!) Isn't it silly to try to preserve old clichés when naturalness and freedom are so much better?

> —*advertisement for* Cosmopolitan *in*
> The New York Times, *1973*

There aren't enough men to go around. . . . Every time there's a plane accident, it's 100 men dead . . . and I literally think, "Why couldn't some *women* have been on that flight?"

> Cosmopolitan *editor* HELEN GURLEY BROWN *in 1982*

My dears, apart from Anatole France and Albert Schweitzer, there is no man interested in anything but sex.

> *British columnist and critic of feminism* BARBARA AMIEL.
> *When she was editor of* The Toronto Sun *in the early*
> *1980s,* Sun *vending boxes bore signs that read, "This is*
> *where you can pick up Barbara Amiel"*

──────────── C O U N T E R P O I N T ────────────

*I became a feminist as an alternative to becoming a
masochist.*

American writer SALLY KEMPTON

───────────────── ◆ ─────────────────

Power [in a man] is an aphrodisiac because it protects and offers a
shield from the world. It envelopes a woman and plays to her most
basic instinct of vulnerability. . . . Power is sexy, not simply in its
own right, but because it inspires self-confidence in its owner and a
shiver of subservience on the part of those who approach it.

BARBARA AMIEL *in a 1986 article for a magazine in her
native Canada, entitled, "Why Women Marry Up." In 1992,
Amiel married Anglo-Canadian press baron Conrad Black*

Anglo-Saxon men are not interested in women. And this is a
problem that needs analysis. I don't know whether it is cultural or
biological, but there is something there that isn't working—that's
obvious. Moreover, I remember from strolling about in London that
men in the streets don't look at you. When you do this in Paris . . . a
workman, or indeed any man, looks at passing women. . . . For a
woman arriving in an Anglo-Saxon country, it is astonishing. She
says to herself, "What is the matter?"

EDITH CRESSON, *first female prime minister of France
from 1991 to 1992, in a 1987 interview*

——————— C O U N T E R P O I N T ———————

I much prefer a nonbeauty with great personality.
fashion designer GIORGIO ARMANI in 1992

————————————— ◆ —————————————

Pursuit and flight are the most erotic moments in the chess game of love, whilst the most vital catalysts between a girl and a boy are mystery and fever.

British novelist CAROLINE KELLET *in 1988*

One good thing came out of the [Gorbachev-Bush] summit. We got to see that Dan Rather is definitely a he-man and no wimp.

American newspaper columnist LIZ SMITH *in 1988 on the CBS anchor's open-at-the-collar shirt while covering the summit*

Ideally a woman should not have a career unless it's necessary for the financial stability of the marriage.

MELISSA SADOFF, *author of* Woman as Chameleon (Or How to be an Ideal Woman), *in 1988*

As far as our physical endurance and how our emotions change every month, I feel there are certain instances that we don't need to be in a place where a man is.

KELLYE CASH, *Miss America 1987, in 1988*

Yes, if ironed sheets mean so much to your husband, it's worth thirty minutes a week to make him happy.

U.S. syndicated newspaper columnist ANN LANDERS

———————— C O U N T E R P O I N T ————————

Men build bridges and throw railroads across deserts, and yet they contend successfully that the job of sewing on a button is beyond them. Accordingly, they don't have to sew buttons.

American writer HEYWOOD BROWN

————————————— ◆ —————————————

Feminism is a failed ideology that produces women who are burned-out and bitter.

PHYLLIS SCHLAFLY, *anti-feminist activist, in 1988*

I don't think women are interesting. I have many women friends, but I don't feel a pressing need for their company.

actress OLIVIA DE HAVILLAND *in 1988*

A man should be the head of the household. And if a woman has any brains, she can usually lead him around by the nose.

actress JANE RUSSELL *in 1988*

It was the first female-style revolution: no violence and we all went shopping.

GLORIA STEINEM *in 1989, on the fall of the Berlin Wall*

I loved the danger. He was so exciting. I can't describe it. He was a turn-on. I think what people don't realize with a certain type of woman that there are times when she wants the man she's with to be . . . a man.

> ROBIN GIVENS *in 1989 on her relationship with boxer Mike Tyson*

───────────── **COUNTERPOINT** ─────────────

One of the things about equality is not just that you be treated equally to a man, but that you treat yourself equally to the way you treat a man.

actress MARLO THOMAS

───────────── ◆ ─────────────

This way the girlfriend can go through the drive-through and pay her respects in whatever name she chooses, while the wife is inside with the deceased. It happens all the time.

> LAFAYETTE GATLING *in 1989, describing the drive-through feature of her Chicago funeral home, where there are closed-circuit TVs for viewing bodies*

Women's lib says you must be free, but free from what? I've traveled all over the world and have never met a man of any class, creed, color or nationality who wants to go into a room with the woman who is his wife and mother to his children and wonder how many other men have gone to bed with her.

> *British romance writer* BARBARA CARTLAND *in 1989*

───────────── C O U N T E R P O I N T ─────────────

People call me a feminist whenever I express sentiments that differentiate me from a doormat or a prostitute.
REBECCA WEST, British writer and critic
(1893–1983)

──────────────── ◆ ────────────────

It was put in my checking account for me and I just spent it, and when it was gone, I waited for next week. All I know is I got it and I spent it like any woman would.
TAMMY FAYE BAKKER, *wife of former televangelist Jim Bakker, on her spending habits, in 1989*

I don't think independence is good for you. It's more difficult and courageous to be dependent on a man.
ISABELLA MACKEY, *founding member of the Campaign for the Feminine Woman, in 1989*

The battle for women's rights has been largely won.
MARGARET THATCHER *in 1982*

───────────── C O U N T E R P O I N T ─────────────

If women want any rights more than they have, why don't they just take them, and not be talking about it.
abolitionist SOJOURNER TRUTH in 1863

──────────────── ◆ ────────────────

Feminism is doomed to failure because it is based on an attempt to repeal and restructure human nature.

PHYLLIS SCHLAFLY *in 1989*

Sexual harassment on the job is not a problem for virtuous women.

PHYLLIS SCHLAFLY

She was saying, "You son of a [expletive]; you [expletive] can't do this to me; I'm a doctor. I hope you [expletive] get shot and come into my hospital so I can refuse to treat you, or if any other trooper gets shot, I will also refuse to treat them."

a Virginia state trooper describing the arrest in 1990 of Geraldine Richter, an orthopedic surgeon who convinced a judge that her erratic behavior was caused by premenstrual syndrome, not drunkenness

I haven't read *War and Peace*, but that's a man's book anyway.

KAYE GIBBONS, *author of* A Virtuous Woman, *in 1990*

Let your husband feel he is the boss. And never have a best friend— they always try to seduce your husband!

British romance novelist BARBARA CARTLAND *in 1990*

Yes, I do. And I always defer to him, too.

ABIGAIL VAN BUREN (*Dear Abby*), *advice columnist, when asked in 1990 if she caters to her husband*

─────────────── C O U N T E R P O I N T ───────────────

We don't see things as they are, we see them as we are.
ANAÏS NIN, American writer (1903–1977)

──────────────── ◆ ────────────────

What began as a movement of eccentric individualists has turned into an ideology that attracts weak personalities who are looking for something to believe in.
author and critic of feminists CAMILLE PAGLIA *in 1992*

Guys make passes at me and blow whistles at me. I just throw it off my back. I don't think anything of it. That's the way it is. If someone raped me, that's a different story.
game-show hostess VANNA WHITE *in 1991, elaborating on her belief that the sexual harassment charges against Clarence Thomas were "blown way out of proportion"*

─────────────── C O U N T E R P O I N T ───────────────

Women are repeatedly accused of taking things personally. I cannot see any other honest way of taking them.
MARYA MANNES, American writer

──────────────── ◆ ────────────────

How he looks in a bathing suit should not be discounted. The fact is, I stare at men quite a lot.
actress JANE FONDA *in 1991, when asked what parts of a man are the biggest turn-on*

I am convinced that, even without restrictions, there still would have been no female Pascal, Milton, or Kant. . . . If civilization had been left in female hands, we would still be living in grass huts.

CAMILLE PAGLIA *in 1991*

─────────── **COUNTERPOINT** ───────────

The women's liberation movement really had a profound effect on this whole country. I think you should call it a men's liberation movement because it liberated men, because it opened our eyes and our ears and our hearts. It liberated us from our own stereotypes. I think that the women's movement made men better.

A. M. ROSENTHAL, columnist, in
The New York Times, 1992

──────────── ◆ ────────────

We are unimportant. We are here to serve, to heal the wounds, and to give love. We want men . . . to look after us.

MARIKE DE KLERK, *wife of South African president
F. W. de Klerk, in 1991*

Models are like baseball players. We make a lot of money quickly, but all of a sudden we're thirty years old, we don't have a college education, we're qualified for nothing, and we're used to a very nice lifestyle. The best thing is to marry a movie star.

CINDY CRAWFORD, *American fashion model, in 1992*

─────────── C O U N T E R P O I N T ───────────

Why is the careless, easy-going, irresponsible way of the young girl so attractive to men? It does not make for domestic happiness; and why, or why, oh why, do some of our best men marry such odd little sticks of pinhead women, with a brain similar in calibre to a second-rate butterfly, while the most intelligent, unselfish, and womanly women are left unmated? I am going to ask about this the first morning I am in heaven.

Canadian feminist and politician
NELLIE MCCLUNG

────────────── ◆ ──────────────

A smart girl is one who knows how to play tennis, piano, and dumb.
actress LYNN REDGRAVE *in 1992*

A home is a man's castle . . . and nobody can do more to ensure this than the woman. Simply put, she can make it heaven or hell for him to come home to at day's end, and in so doing contribute to heaven or hell on earth for herself.
Tennessee circuit court judge MURIEL ROBINSON-RICE *in 1992*

[I'm] just going on in my dumb way, having fun and being helpful.
First Lady BARBARA BUSH *on the campaign trail in 1992, waving off her own achievements and popularity in order to ward off the ill effects of the so-called "Hillary Factor"—that is, being too bright to be First Lady*

──────────── C O U N T E R P O I N T ────────────

"I hate discussions of feminism that end up with who does the dishes," she said. So do I. But at the end, there are always the damned dishes.

MARILYN FRENCH, *The Women's Room*

──────────── ◆ ────────────

I think there's a lot of jealousy and competitiveness between women, because I got much better reviews from men than women. The women's reviews were very vitriolic and petty.

BARBRA STREISAND, *responding to assessments of her directorial work on* The Prince of Tides *in 1992*

Most women do not want to be liberated from their essential natures as women.

MARILYN QUAYLE, *explaining her decision to abandon thoughts of a law career in favor of being a full-time homemaker, to the Republican National Convention in 1992*

──────────── C O U N T E R P O I N T ────────────

The phrase "working mother" is redundant.

JANE SELLMAN, 20th-century American writer

──────────── ◆ ────────────

Total victory—none of this litmus-test, big-tent garbage.

> PHYLLIS SCHLAFLY *in 1992, explaining why she approved of the G.O.P.'s anti-feminist, anti-gay, anti-environment platform—a reversal of the inclusionary "big tent" efforts by the party's late chairman Lee Atwater, who had sought in 1988 to reach beyond the G.O.P.'s conservative wing to moderate voters*

I don't work well with women—especially conceited, stuck-up women. I work better with men. I'm a man's woman, not a woman's woman, thank God.

> *actress* DEBRA WINGER *in 1992*

I always tell my girls: think like a man, but act and look like a woman.

> CAROL HEISS, *figure-skating coach, in 1992*

Ask us about our cup size or our favorite position, but—please—no personal questions.

> *model* SHANE BARBI *in 1992, who appeared with identical sister Sia on a* Playboy *cover, when asked which sister is older*

COUNTERPOINT

One is not born a woman, one becomes one.
> SIMONE DE BEAUVOIR, French writer and philosopher, (1908–1986)

◆

We're both victims of prom-queen syndrome. I got over it with the first wrinkle, but Gennifer is still reaching for that tiara.

> JOY HOWLAND *in 1992, on her partying days with Gennifer Flowers, who alleged an affair with Bill Clinton*

How dare you! With all that is in me, I resent your caustic remark.

> TAMMY WYNETTE, *American country singer, in a 1992 letter to Hillary Clinton, who in responding to the Flowers allegation had defended her husband but said she was "not sitting here like some little woman standing by her man like Tammy Wynette." She later apologized to Wynette.*

She felt herself being lured into the thrilling undertow of her old passion to own, to possess, to acquire.

> *shopping-as-sex, described in* JUDITH KRANTZ's *1992 novel,* Scruples Two

They don't have a page that broad.

> GENNIFER FLOWERS *in 1992, after posing nude for* Penthouse *magazine, on why Hillary Clinton couldn't "bare her butt in any magazine"*

─────────────── **C O U N T E R P O I N T** ───────────────

[I'm no different from] every woman who gets up in the morning and gets breakfast for her family and goes off to a job of any sort, where she assumes a different role for the hours she's at work, who runs out at lunch to buy material for a costume for her daughter or to buy invitations for a party that she's going to have and after work goes and picks up her children and then maybe goes out with her husband: our lives are a mixture of these different roles.

HILLARY RODHAM CLINTON in 1993,
describing life in the White House
with husband Bill and daughter Chelsea

─────────────── ◆ ───────────────

Michael's not emotional. He doesn't take it personally if I correct him. And he never has P.M.S.

NBC executive DANELLE BLACK, *on her male secretary in 1992*

[She's] a parent-pleasing, teacher-pleasing little kiss-ass.

CAMILLE PAGLIA *on Naomi Wolf, author of*
The Beauty Myth

I'm not sure we should get rid of your cellulite—it may be all that's holding you together.

cartoon caption of a male doctor speaking to a female patient in Good Housekeeping's *January 1993 issue*

·4·

The Bully Pulpit

Such is the stupidity of woman's character that it is incumbent upon her, in every particular, to distrust herself and obey her husband.

CONFUCIUS, *c. 500* B.C.

It is the law of nature that woman should be held under the dominance of man.

CONFUCIUS, *c. 500* B.C.

Nothing so much casts down the mind of man from its citadel as do the blandishments of women, and that physical contact without which a wife cannot be possessed.

ST. AUGUSTINE, *c. A.D. 387*

─────────── C O U N T E R P O I N T ───────────

In passing, also, I would like to say that the first time Adam had a chance he laid the blame on woman.
        NANCY ASTOR, *British politician (1879–1964)*

───────────── ◆ ─────────────

A man should be careful not to pass between two women, two dogs or two swine.

ancient Hebrew saying

There is no female so modest that she will not be stirred with passion at the advances of a stranger.
        SIR JOHN OF SALISBURY, *Bishop of Chartres from 1176 to 1180, in 1159*

God foresaw that woman would be an occasion of sin to man. Therefore He should not have made woman. . . . It was necessary for woman to be made, as the Scripture says, as a *helper* to man; not, indeed, as a helpmate in other works, as some say, since man can be more efficiently helped by another man in other works; but as a helper in the work of generation.
        ST. THOMAS AQUINAS in Summa theologica, *1267–1273*

In her particular nature, woman is defective and misbegotten, for the active force in the male seed tends to the production of a perfect likeness in the masculine sex; while the production of woman is due to a weakness in the generative force or imperfection in the pre-existing matter or even from some external influences, for example, the humid winds from the south.

ST. THOMAS AQUINAS, *Italian philosopher* (*1225?–1274*)

The words of the Torah should be burned rather than taught to women.

Talmud, Sotah 3:4, c. A.D. *1501*

No good ever came out of female domination. God created Adam master and lord of all living creatures, but Eve spoiled all.

MARTIN LUTHER *in 1532*

─────────── C O U N T E R P O I N T ───────────

If the first woman God ever made was strong enough to turn the world upside down all alone, these women together ought to be able to turn it back, and get it right side up again! And now they is asking to do it, the men better let them.

abolitionist SOJOURNER TRUTH (1797–1883)

──────────────── ◆ ────────────────

Eloquence in women shouldn't be praised; it is more fitting for them to lisp and stammer. This is more becoming to them.

MARTIN LUTHER *in 1538*

─────────── **COUNTERPOINT** ───────────

Men are taught to apologize for their weaknesses, women for their strengths.

LOIS WAYNE, American advertising executive

──────────────── ◆ ────────────────

The spiritual direction of just three women is a task more arduous than the administration of an entire Order.

ST. IGNATIUS LOYOLA, *founder of the Jesuit Order, in 1548*

Nature doth paint them further to be weak, frail, impatient, feeble and foolish; and experience hath declared them to be unconstant, variable, cruel and lacking the spirit of counsel.

JOHN KNOX, *Scottish theologian, in 1560*

Intellect in a woman is unbecoming.

CARDINAL RICHELIEU (*Armand Jean du Plessis*) *French religious administrator and statesman* (1585–1642)

False also and harmful to Christian education is the so-called method of "co-education." . . . There is not in nature itself, which fashions the two quite different in organism, in temperament, in abilities, anything to suggest that there can be or ought to be promiscuity, and much less equality, in the training of the two sexes.

POPE PIUS XI *in 1929*

I want to remind young women that motherhood is the vocation of women . . . It is women's eternal vocation.

POPE JOHN PAUL II *in 1979*

As a recommended caution, a woman must stand behind a man and the place of her prostration be located a little behind that of the man.

AYATOLLAH KHAMENEI, *Iranian theologian and dictator, in 1980*

Architecturally the church is laid out in the shape of a cross. To me it looks like an inverted phallus, with the two pulpits on the crossbar as testicles.

NANCY JACKMAN *writing in* Toronto *magazine in 1986*

When you help the shepherd, you're helping the sheep.

televangelist JIM BAKKER *in 1980, speaking to disciple Jessica Hahn in a Florida motel room. The conversation would spell the demise of Bakker's PTL organization when it became public in 1987*

I think it's a legitimate question: Are you now or recently have you been running around with a bunch of bimbos?

presidential candidate and televangelist PAT ROBERTSON *in 1988, calling into question the marital fidelity of his political rivals*

Women are to take care of the family.

SPENCER W. KIMBALL, *past president of the Mormon church, in 1988*

——————— C O U N T E R P O I N T ———————

Can we today measure devotion to husband and children by our indifference to everything else?

GOLDA MEIR

———————————— ◆ ————————————

People can be spiritually randy and if you take Communion you should accept that you swallow the body of Christ: hair, genitals— the lot.

WENDY PERRIAM *writing in* The Scotsman *in 1989*

We have to be careful that their tender hearts do not play tricks on them.

EDOUARD CARDINAL GAGNON, *head of the Vatican's Pontifical Council for the Family, in 1989, on his reservations about women serving on U.S. panels deciding annulments*

A woman carrying a Torah is like a pig at the Wailing Wall.

MEIR YEHUDA GETZ, *Orthodox rabbi in charge of Judaism's holiest shrine, the Wailing Wall, in 1990*

Feminists and all these radical gals—most of them are failures. They've blown it. Some of them have been married, but they married some Casper Milquetoast who asked permission to go to the bathroom. These women just need a man in the house. That's all they need. Most of these feminists need a man to tell them what time of day it is and to lead them home. And they blew it and they're mad at all men. Feminists hate men. They're sexist . . . that's their problem.

televangelist JERRY FALWELL *in 1991*

It is my opinion that the . . . ever-increasing number of mothers out of the home and in the workplace is the root cause of many of the problems of delinquency, drugs, and gangs—both male and female.

GORDON HINCKLEY, *first counselor in the first presidency of the Church of Jesus Christ of Latter-day Saints, in 1992*

◆5◆

Political Affairs

Promoting a woman to regiment [rule], superiorite, dominion, or empire above any realme, nation or citie is repugnant to nature, contumelie to God, a thing most contrarious to His revealed will and approved ordinance; and finallie it is the subversion of good order, of all equitie and justice.

JOHN KNOX *in 1558*

I must not write a word to you about politics, because you are a woman.

JOHN ADAMS *to his wife Abigail*

The appointment of a woman to office is an innovation for which the public is not prepared, nor am I.

THOMAS JEFFERSON *in 1807*

We are obliged to go fair and softly and, in practice, you know we are the subjects. We have only the name of masters, and rather than give up this, which would completely subject us to the despotism of the petticoat, I hope General Washington and all our brave heroes would fight.

> JOHN ADAMS *in a jesting reply to a letter from his wife*
> *Abigail written in March 1776: "In the new code of laws*
> *which I suppose it will be necessary for you to make, I desire*
> *you would remember the ladies and be more generous and*
> *favorable to them than your ancestors. Do not put unlimited*
> *power into the hands of the husbands. Remember, all men*
> *would be tyrants, if they could. If particular care and*
> *attention is not paid to the ladies, we are determined to*
> *foment a rebellion, and will not hold ourselves bound by any*
> *laws in which we have no voice or representation. That your*
> *sex are naturally tyrannical is a truth so thoroughly*
> *established as to admit of no dispute."*

───────── **COUNTERPOINT** ─────────

The queens in history compare favorably with the kings.
ELIZABETH CADY STANTON and SUSAN
B. ANTHONY in *History of Woman Suffrage*

───────────── ◆ ─────────────

Men and women differ much as animals and plants do. Men and animals correspond, as do women and plants, for women develop more placidly and always retain the formless indeterminate unity of feeling and sentiment. When women have control over the government, the state is plunged into peril, for they do not act according to the standards of universality, but are influenced by random inclinations and opinions.

GEORG WILHELM FRIEDRICH HEGEL *in 1821*

Sensible and responsible women do not want to vote.

GROVER CLEVELAND, *American statesman, in 1905*

Even if every woman in the land should exercise the suffrage, the votes of the thoughtful and conscientious would almost certainly be largely outweighed by those of the disreputable, the ignorant, the thoughtless, the purchased and the coerced. . . . This phase of the suffrage question cannot better be presented than in the following words of another: "Women change politics less than politics change women."

GROVER CLEVELAND *in 1905*

─────────── C O U N T E R P O I N T ───────────

The true republic: men, their rights and nothing more;
women, their rights and nothing less.

Suffragette SUSAN B. ANTHONY (1820–1906)

───────────── ◆ ─────────────

─────────────── C O U N T E R P O I N T ───────────────

Into the women's keeping is committed the destiny of the generations to come after us.

THEODORE ROOSEVELT

──────────────── ◆ ────────────────

The grant of the Parliamentary franchise to women in this country would be a political mistake of a very disastrous kind.

HERBERT ASQUITH, *British prime minister. Asquith impressed writer Rebecca West as "undistinguished in his crimes, expedited by his clumsy thwackings of women from behind the bars of authority."*

─────────────── C O U N T E R P O I N T ───────────────

The history of men's opposition to women's emancipation is more interesting perhaps than the story of emancipation itself.

VIRGINIA WOOLF in 1933

──────────────── ◆ ────────────────

The grant of suffrage to women is repugnant to instincts that strike their roots deep in the order of nature. It runs counter to human reason, it flouts the teachings of experience and the admonitions of common sense.

editorial in The New York Times, *1915*

──────── **C O U N T E R P O I N T** ────────

Women who set a low value on themselves make life hard for all women.

NELLIE MCCLUNG, Canadian suffragist and
reformer (1873–1951)

──────── ◆ ────────

The greatest thing for any woman to be is a wife and mother.

THEODORE ROOSEVELT, *American statesman*

Warren, it's lucky you weren't born a girl, because you can't say no.

U.S. President WARREN G. HARDING's *father speaking to
him after the Teapot Dome scandal, in which Harding's
political associates—the "Ohio gang"—extracted lucrative
favors from the government*

──────── **C O U N T E R P O I N T** ────────

*I have been asked whether there are any intelligent women in
America. There must be; for politically the men there are
such futile gossips that the United States could not possibly
carry on unless there were some sort of practical intelligence
back of them.*

GEORGE BERNARD SHAW in 1928

──────── ◆ ────────

We're well aware of the male homosexual problem in this country, which is of course minor, but to our certain knowledge there is not one lesbian in England.

> LORD CHAMBERLAIN *of England to Lillian Hellman*
> *during a discussion of her play* The Children's Hour

Women are hard enough to handle now, without giving them a gun.

> *Senator* BARRY GOLDWATER *of Arizona in 1980,*
> *arguing against women in the armed forces*

Three things have been difficult to tame: the oceans, fools and women. We may soon be able to tame the ocean; fools and women will take a little longer.

> *U.S. Vice-President* SPIRO AGNEW *in 1970. Agnew was forced to resign in 1973 over conflict-of-interest charges*

Like most women, my wife thinks with her glands, not with her head.

> *Senator* MARK HATFIELD *of Oregon in 1974*

——————— C O U N T E R P O I N T ———————

If there were enough women in Parliament, the Health Ministry would become more important than that of Finance.
GORDON BATES, physician and founder of the Health League of Canada, in 1941

———————————— ◆ ————————————

Women are to have fun with. In politics, I prefer not to see a woman. Instead of getting all worked up, they should stay as they are—like flowers.

> *Polish political leader* LECH WALESA *in 1981. A decade later, a dramatic turnaround in the lagging Polish economy was spearheaded by Walesa's prime minister Hanna Suchocka*

Anyone who knows Dan Quayle knows he would rather play golf than have sex any day.

> MARILYN QUAYLE, *responding to suggestions that her husband had conducted an extramarital affair in the early 1980s*

——————— C O U N T E R P O I N T ———————

*That's the way I feel about men, too. I only hope for your
sake that you haven't been disappointed as often as I have.*
MILLICENT FENWICK, New Jersey
congresswoman, during a debate over equal
rights for women, responding to a male
legislator who had said: "I just don't like this
amendment. I've always thought of women as
kissable, cuddly and smelling good."

——————————— ◆ ———————————

Damn it, when you get married, you kind of expect you're going to
get a little sex.

JEREMIAH DENTON, *Alabama senator, in 1981,
commenting on the prosecution of a man charged
with raping his wife*

If it wasn't for women, us men would still be walking around in skin
suits carrying clubs.

RONALD REAGAN *in 1983, addressing a
convention of women's organizations*

[Women are] less equipped psychologically to "stay the course" in the
brawling arenas of business, commerce, industry and the professions.

PATRICK BUCHANAN, *American journalist, in a 1983 column*

─────────────── C O U N T E R P O I N T ───────────────

People have been writing premature obituaries on the women's movement since its beginning.

columnist ELLEN GOODMAN

──────────────────── ◆ ────────────────────

What really causes marital abuse is small families. If all women had a lot of brothers, this would never take place.

Iowa State Representative CHARLES PONCY

Human beings are not animals, and I do not want to see sex and sexual differences treated as casually and amorally as dogs and other beasts treat them. I believe this could happen under the ERA.

RONALD REAGAN, *speaking against the Equal Rights Amendment in the 1980s*

─────────────── C O U N T E R P O I N T ───────────────

Do you know, it is not praise that does me good, but when men speak ill of me, then, with a noble assurance I say to myself, as I smile at them, "let us be revenged by proving them to be liars."

CATHERINE II, 18th-century Empress of Russia

──────────────────── ◆ ────────────────────

You could call them Fritz and Tits because then there'd be three boobs in the White House . . . Geraldine Ferraro! Big deal, let's put a woman in the White House. May I just tell you something? Can we talk here for a second? It's no big deal to have a woman in the White House. John F. Kennedy had a thousand of them.

> *comedian and talk-show host* JOAN RIVERS *at a 1984 G.O.P. fundraiser, ridiculing the Democratic presidential ticket of Walter (Fritz) Mondale and Geraldine Ferraro*

There was a time in my life when I spent ninety percent of my money on booze and broads. And the rest of it I just wasted.

> *Georgia congressman* BEN JONES, *former star of the TV series* The Dukes of Hazzard

———————————— C O U N T E R P O I N T ————————————

> *I thought about running as a man, but I decided against it.*
> AUDREY MCLAUGHLIN, leader of Canada's New Democratic Party, explaining in a 1992 autobiography why she opted not to take on a more abrasive attitude in order to win her party's leadership

———————————— ◆ ————————————

Get that whore off my chair.

> *attributed to Republican senator* STEVE SIMMS *of Idaho, directed at a female TV reporter who was critical of him in her coverage*

Who'd you sleep with to get your job?
> JON PECK, *press secretary to Florida governor Bob Martinez,*
> *to a female* Miami Herald *reporter*

Just calm down, baby.
> *Canadian justice minister* JOHN CROSBIE *in a House of Commons*
> *barb directed at opposition member Sheila Copps. Crosbie was minister*
> *responsible for the Status of Women at the time.*

A woman's place is in the bedroom.
> *Philippine president* FERDINAND MARCOS *in 1986*

The proper role of a mother with a child two years old is to devote herself to that child.
> *Senator* GORDON HUMPHREY *in 1988 on the electoral bid*
> *of Congressional candidate Betty Tamposi*

COUNTERPOINT

When you want anything said, ask a man. If you want anything done, ask a woman.

> MARGARET THATCHER

◆

From the point of view of nature, there can be no equality between men and women in character or temperament, in moral or physical strength.
> *Libyan president* MUAMMAR GADHAFI *in 1988*

Are you hot to trot this week?

> *Virginia state senator* HUNTER ANDREWS *in 1988,*
> *to a female reporter*

To demand equality between [a woman and a man] in any dirty work that stains her beauty and detracts from her femininity is unjust and cruel.

> MUAMMAR GADHAFI *in 1988*

After years of effort, women have won the right to be taken more seriously than they deserve.

> STANLEY BING, *pseudonym for American financial writer*
> *and* Esquire *columnist*

─────────── **COUNTERPOINT** ───────────

It's all sorts of middle-aged white men in suits—forests of middle-aged men in dark suits. All slightly red-faced from eating and drinking too much.

> DIANE ABBOTT, the only black woman member of
> the British parliament, on her colleagues in 1988

───────────── ◆ ─────────────

I have it on firsthand source that beneath Barbara Bush's maternalistic exterior lies a Bombshell Beige blonde who tones her hair silver with Clairol's Shimmer Lights shampoo so that people will take her seriously.

> *Nancy Reagan's hairdresser* ROBIN WEIR *in 1988*

Why you got your boob covered up?

> ERNEST KONNYU, *Republican congressman from California, to a 26-year-old female aide. Konnyu later tried to extricate himself from controversy by saying, "At the conference she wore her name tag . . . right over her boobs . . . I don't think it was right for her to have her name tag on in a—it should be up high. She's not exactly heavily stacked, okay? . . . So I told her . . . to move the darn name tag off her boobs." Konnyu was defeated in 1988.*

Republicans understand the importance of bondage between mother and child.

> *former vice-president* DAN QUAYLE, *in an apparent reference to mother-and-child bonding*

She has a very major cause and a very major interest that is a very complex and consuming issue with her. And that's me.

> DAN QUAYLE, *asked in 1989 if his wife Marilyn was planning to take up a cause*

Women make the best cooks and housewives and should be encouraged in that role.

> *British Columbia premier* WILLIAM VANDER ZALM *in 1989*

───────────── C O U N T E R P O I N T ─────────────

I am extraordinarily patient, provided I get my way in the end.

> MARGARET THATCHER

───────────────── ◆ ─────────────────

If everybody in this town connected with politics had to leave town because of [chasing women] and drinking, you'd have no government.
Senator BARRY GOLDWATER *in 1989*

You're grown, she's grown, and you're both single. Now you may be a faggot or something, and that sounds strange.
Congressman GUS SAVAGE, *Democrat of Illinois, in 1989, on accusations of sexually assaulting a Peace Corps volunteer*

Do you know why God created woman? Because sheep can't type.
KENNETH ARMBRISTER, *Texas state senator, in 1989*

One of the first recommendations was that I do something about my teeth—they were too crooked. Another theme was that my eyebrows were too dark. Some people wanted to change my hair. A lot of people didn't like my clothes.
AUDREY MCLAUGHLIN, *leader of Canada's New Democratic Party, on the image advice she received from colleagues after becoming party leader in 1989*

──────────── COUNTERPOINT ────────────

If I don't feel like wearing a bra I don't wear one. I'd never let my nipples show at a state function—I'd be frightened the old men would have heart attacks.

MARGARET TRUDEAU

The key to the city would be fine, but I'd like to give her a key to my apartment.

>*Miami Beach, Florida, mayor* ALEX DAOUD *in 1990,*
>*referring to a female police officer*

When I got to thinking, the way we get thoroughbred horses and thoroughbred dogs is through inbreeding. Maybe we would get a supersharp kid.

>*Louisiana legislator* CARL GUNTER *in 1990, on why he*
>*thinks incest is not a valid reason for an abortion*

I say this a lot, and I probably shouldn't: the difference between rape and seduction is salesmanship.

>BILL CARPENTER, *mayor of Independence, Missouri, in 1990*

The weather is like rape: if it's inevitable, just relax and enjoy it.

>CLAYTON WILLIAMS *in conversation with reporters during a*
>*sudden turn in the weather during his unsuccessful Texas*
>*gubernatorial campaign in 1990*

I could take this home, Marilyn. This is something teenage boys might find of interest.

>*Former vice-president* DAN QUAYLE *in 1990, moments*
>*before buying a South American Indian doll that, when lifted,*
>*displays an erection. Marilyn, attempting to avoid a public-*
>*relations disaster, tried unsuccessfully to prevent the purchase,*
>*saying, "Dan, you're not getting that. Oh, no."*

Well, Teddy, I see you've changed your position on offshore drilling.

> *Alabama Senator* HOWELL HEFLIN *in 1990, to Senator Ted
> Kennedy after seeing a photograph of Kennedy in a
> compromising position with a woman while floating in a boat*

Unidentified blonde!

> *Senator* TED KENNEDY *in 1990, to photographers lying in
> wait for him; the woman was his sister Jean Kennedy Smith*

——————————— C O U N T E R P O I N T ———————————

*My advice to the women's clubs of America is to raise more
hell and fewer children.*

> JAMES MCNEILL WHISTLER, American
> painter (1834–1903)

———————————— ◆ ————————————

Vote for Mestrinho. He could be your father.

> *campaign slogan circulated by enemies of Brazilian
> gubernatorial candidate Gilberto Mestrinho, who has fathered
> nine children by four women, in 1990*

——————————— C O U N T E R P O I N T ———————————

*Whatever women do they must do twice as well as men to be
thought half as good. Luckily, this is not difficult.*

> CHARLOTTE WHITTON, mayor of
> Ottawa, Ontario

———————————— ◆ ————————————

Dick and I have something in common. That is that we both overmarried.

> DAN QUAYLE *in 1990, on Defense Secretary Dick Cheney,*
> *whose wife then headed the National Endowment*
> *for the Humanities*

At least we're talking about two consenting adults here, which makes it almost quaint by prevailing Ohio political standards.

> JOE DIRCK, *writer with the Cleveland* Plain Dealer, *on an*
> *alleged affair by Columbus mayor Dana Rinehart in 1990*

That's garbage. Why can't they catch me in a sex scandal?

> *California assembly speaker* WILLIE BROWN *in 1990,*
> *responding to news of an FBI probe into his connection with*
> *a garbage company*

I had an erotic dream about you recently. And those dreams usually come true.

> *Republican political consultant* ROGER STONE
> *to a female acquaintance in 1990*

I am available to make love with Saddam Hussein to achieve peace in the Middle East.

> *Italian parliamentarian and porn star*
> ILONA STALLER *(Cicciolina) in 1990*

[It's] been an unexciting and dull campaign. With me in it, it's no longer dull.

> Ohio Congressman BUZ LUKENS, *convicted of having sexual relations with a minor, on deciding to seek re-election in 1990*

The worst thing I've heard about the Kennedys is that they're very smart but when they get horny, their penis takes over and their brain closes.

> FLORENCE ORBACH, *78, a juror who was rejected as biased at the William Kennedy Smith trial in 1991*

──────────── C O U N T E R P O I N T ────────────

I didn't ignore you, Senator. I chose to refuse to shake your hand.

> BETTY FRIEDAN in 1991, after Senator Alan Simpson tried to shake her hand during a sharply worded talk about the Supreme Court nomination of Clarence Thomas

──────────────── ◆ ────────────────

The truth is no ugly woman can succeed in politics.

> *French prime minister* EDITH CRESSON *in 1991*

We shouldn't be bothered by her. She is just a middle-aged hysteric.

> *Japanese parliamentarian* SHINTARO ISHIHARA *in 1991 on French prime minister Edith Cresson's anti-Japanese remarks*

I believe in the natural family order where the man works and the woman stays home and raises the kids. It's what the people want and what they will get if I am elected governor.

Republican gubernatorial candidate LARRY FORGY *of Kentucky in 1991*

──────────── C O U N T E R P O I N T ────────────

Once in cabinet we had to deal with the fact that there had been an outbreak of assaults on women at night. One minister suggested a curfew: women should stay home after dark. I said, "But it's the men who are attacking the women. If there's to be a curfew, let the men stay home, not the women."

Israeli prime minister GOLDA MEIR in 1974

──────────── ◆ ────────────

I'm thinking about entering politics—I'd love to do it. But I haven't got the right wife.

rock musician MICK JAGGER

You want a wife who's intelligent, but not too intelligent.

RICHARD NIXON *in 1992, offering counsel to presidential candidate Bill Clinton*

I have sacrificed everything in my life that I consider precious in order to advance the political career of my husband.

PAT NIXON, *wife of Richard Nixon*

———————— C O U N T E R P O I N T ————————

I do, and I also wash and iron them.
> DENIS THATCHER, husband of British prime
> minister Margaret Thatcher, when asked who
> wears the pants in his marriage

——————————— ◆ ———————————

Stop being Mr. Nice Guy. When you're nice, it just makes me want to throw up.
> *Minneapolis talk-show host* BARBARA CARLSON *in 1991*
> *to her guest and former husband, Governor Arne Carlson*

She will have to get her ecstasy of orgasm some other way. She will have to achieve that elsewhere—maybe with a vibrator.
> *Nebraska state senator* ERNIE CHAMBERS *in 1991, on*
> *assistant attorney general Sharon Lindgren, who was trying to*
> *get a convicted killer executed*

Basically, we went about the business of making Anita Hill's life a living hell.
> CHRIS WILSON, *New Hampshire youth coordinator for the*
> *Patrick Buchanan presidential campaign, on digging up anti-*
> *Hill dirt while enrolled in 1991 at the University of*
> *Oklahoma Law School, where Hill is a professor*

In Europe, extramarital affairs are considered a sign of good health, a feat.

> *Belgian legislator* JEAN-PIERRE DETREMERIE *in 1992, expressing surprise at Americans' preoccupation with allegations of infidelity directed at Bill Clinton*

――――――― COUNTERPOINT ―――――――

Affairs are all right. Just be insanely careful not to have your husband find out.

HELEN GURLEY BROWN

――――――――― ◆ ―――――――――

The weakest nations in the world are those that had a woman as leader. It doesn't mean that Islam is against women. On the contrary, it respects them and says they are equal to men. But [history shows] that weak nations are led by women.

> *interim Afghanistan president* SIBJHATULLAH MOJADEDI *in 1992 on why he opposes women in leadership roles in Islamic governments*

Now we've got all these men out there worrying that we'll all have P.M.S. on the same day and blow the town up.

> BARBARA CARR, *one of four newly elected city councilwomen in Pacifica, California, in 1992*

I find it fascinating that grown men are hiding behind their women.
> *presidential candidate* ROSS PEROT *in 1992*
> *after being criticized by Marilyn Quayle*

—————— COUNTERPOINT ——————

*I suppose I could have stayed home and baked cookies and
had teas, but what I decided to do is fulfill my profession. The
work that I have done as a professional, a public advocate,
has been aimed . . . to assure that women can make the
choices . . . whether it's a full-time career, full-time
motherhood, or some combination.*
> HILLARY RODHAM CLINTON on the campaign
> trail in 1992

——————◆——————

Young man, I want to see you after this rally.
> BILL CLINTON *in 1992 to an Iowa supporter bearing a*
> *placard that read, "Hillary is a babe."*

I am delighted with some of the women that our [Republican] Senate
candidates are going to be taking on because they will be easier to
beat.
> GEORGE BUSH *campaigning for re-election in 1992*

In our family, I'm the boss.
> BORIS YELTSIN *in 1992, asked during a press conference*
> *about the influence on him by his wife Naina*

They're trying to prove their manhood.

> ROSS PEROT *in 1992, on two female reporters*
> *who attempted to ask him tough questions*

I don't think we should have to have them wandering the streets frightening women and people.

> *presidential candidate* PATRICK BUCHANAN *in 1992 on the*
> *need to lock up homeless people who aren't in shelters*

──────── C O U N T E R P O I N T ────────

*If George Bush reminds many women of their first husbands,
Pat Buchanan reminds women why an increasing number of
them are staying single.*

JUDY PEARSON, professor of interpersonal
communications at Ohio University, in 1992

───────────── ◆ ─────────────

I was incoherent and radical. I was even a *feminist*, and I'm very
embarrassed about it. . . . If you grow up as a Jew and a woman in
New York City, you are a liberal until you go away and think things
through.

LISA SCHIFFREN, *speechwriter for Dan Quayle who wrote
his 1992 attack on the TV series character Murphy Brown*

I don't think [women are] temperamentally adjusted to executive
positions. They come at problems from a different direction than men
do. Women, in my estimation, don't see the practical effect of what
they do. . . . Do you want the government to be run by your mother?

PHIL MARCUSE, *campaigning in 1992 for executive of
Oakland County, Michigan, on the lack of qualifications of
his female opponent*

I never imagined I'd be sleeping with a sixty-year-old woman.

Wyoming Senator ALAN SIMPSON *in 1992,
at his wife's birthday party*

You know women, they get moody. . . . You know what the female race is like. Some days aren't as good for them as others—same as some men.

> *Alberta legislator* DOUG CHERRY *in 1992, on why he withheld support from Nancy Betkowski in her bid for the province's Conservative Party leadership*

They seem to be saying, "Here, I've got breasts. Vote for me."
> *former Pennsylvania Democratic Party chairman* LARRY YATCH *in 1992, on the abundance of female political candidates in the so-called "Year of the Woman"*

─────────── **C O U N T E R P O I N T** ───────────

I think it's about time we voted for senators with breasts.
After all, we've been voting for boobs long enough.
> CLAIRE SARGENT *of Arizona in 1992,*
> campaigning against incumbent Senator
> John McCain

───────────── ♦ ─────────────

If that man becomes President, I'll never have to work again.
> *remark attributed in 1992 to* GENNIFER FLOWERS, *who expected to reap fortune from her newfound celebrity as Clinton's self-described mistress*

If we disagree and I think I'm right, I just go on and do what I think is right. And then she tells me, "I told you so."

> BILL CLINTON *in 1992, describing his working relationship*
> *with wife Hillary*

———————————— C O U N T E R P O I N T ————————————

I'll do anything you want, but I won't dye my hair, change my wardrobe or lose weight.

> BARBARA BUSH telling her husband's
> campaign media adviser Roger Ailes what she
> would and would not do to help Bush in his
> 1988 bid for the presidency. In contrast,
> Hillary Rodham Clinton subjected herself to
> a wardrobe makeover, dropped her maiden
> name and, in the 1992 presidential
> campaign, fell mute on the campaign trail to
> present a non-distracting image in service to
> her husband's political aspirations.

———————————— ◆ ————————————

Hell hath no fury like a hooker with a press agent.

> FRANK SINATRA's *response when asked in 1975 about*
> *Judith Campbell Exner's assertion that it was Sinatra who*
> *introduced her to John F. Kennedy, with whom she is alleged*
> *to have had an affair*

──────────── C O U N T E R P O I N T ────────────

Women are being considered as candidates for Vice-president of the United States because it is the worst job in America. It's amazing that men will take it. A job with real power is First Lady. I'd be willing to run for that.

NORA EPHRON

──────────── ◆ ────────────

──────────── C O U N T E R P O I N T ────────────

She's better at organizing and leading people from a complex beginning to a certain end than anybody I've ever worked with in my life.

President BILL CLINTON of his wife, Hillary Rodham Clinton, on the occasion of naming her to head his health care task force in January 1993

──────────── ◆ ────────────

·6·

Annals of Commerce

In point of morals the average woman is, even for business, too crooked.

> STEPHEN LEACOCK, *Canadian economist and writer*
> *(1869–1944)*

I think that a man, somehow or other, can handle business better than we do.

> *actress* EVA GABOR

───────────── COUNTERPOINT ─────────────

Dear, never forget one little point: It's my business. You just work here.

> cosmetics magnate ELIZABETH ARDEN,
> to her husband

───────────────── ◆ ─────────────────

When the day comes that American Express Company has to hire a female employee, it will close its doors.

> JAMES CONGDELL FARGO, *president of American Express,*
> *1881–1914*

Brigands demand your money or your life; women require both.

> NICHOLAS MURRAY BUTLER

[Charles] Revson said women all hope to get laid, and I agree. They're sensuous. They're different from men. They dress to please men. You're not selling utility. That's why uptight women stockbrokers will put on a G-string when they get home. Like Revson said, we're selling hope in a bottle.

> LESLIE WEXNER, *CEO of The Limited, owner of the*
> *Victoria's Secret lingerie chain, in 1985*

I'm a double-B girl in a high-yield world/Drexel, Drexel, Drexel.

> MADONNA, *singing a 1986 promotional video commissioned*
> *by Drexel Burnham Lambert trader Michael Milken, pioneer*
> *of junk-bond financing and convicted on insider-trading charges*

Heaven is an American salary, a Chinese cook, an English house, and a Japanese wife. Hell is defined as having a Chinese salary, an English cook, a Japanese house, and an American wife.

> JAMES H. KABLER III, *chairman of Nikkai Industries Ltd., in 1988*

―――――――――― **COUNTERPOINT** ――――――――

Women's place is in the house, and that's where she should go just as soon as she leaves the office.

      Canadian parliamentarian SHEILA COPPS in 1986

――――――――――――― ◆ ―――――――――――――

We don't need a woman who's an expert in fashion.

      FRED HARTLEY, *chairman of Unocal Corporation, on why there are no women on the company's board, in 1988*

I'm old enough to be grandfather to some of the girls I take out. But why not? They're decorative, they have keen senses of humor. I don't want every dinner conversation to be about what people think of Muammar Kadhafi.

      ROBERT FOMAN, *former chairman of brokerage E. F. Hutton, in 1989*

―――――――――― **COUNTERPOINT** ――――――――

When a man gets up to speak, people listen, then look. When a woman gets up, people look; then if they like what they see, they listen.

      PAULINE FREDERICK, American journalist
      (1908–1990)

――――――――――――― ◆ ―――――――――――――

What could be a more perfect gift for Mother's Day than a book? It won't shed leaves or droop. It can't make her fat and she certainly doesn't need to water it.

> *advertising leaflet distributed by the U.K.'s Book Marketing*
> *Council in 1989 to promote the purchase of books as*
> *Mother's Day presents in place of chocolates*
> *and other traditional gifts*

You don't build a company like this with lace on your underwear.

> Fortune *magazine advertisement for an article on "America's*
> *Toughest Bosses" in 1989*

Operating a hotel is, I think, a woman's business. It's knowing food, keeping a room clean—it's running a house on a larger scale.

> *hotelier* LEONA HELMSLEY *in 1990*

Wall Street is stress, highly emotional, and loaded with rejection. You have to be able to survive that. That's perhaps why women haven't achieved the record that they have in other areas.

> JAMES E. CAYNE, *president of brokerage*
> *Bear Stearns & Co. Inc., in 1990*

──────── **C O U N T E R P O I N T** ────────

*I'm not doing this out of the goodness of my heart. I'm
selfish. I want the very best people I can get. A lot of them
happen to be women.*

RONALD COMPTON, CEO of Aetna Life & Casualty,
in 1992, explaining why he oversaw a personnel
development program that has resulted in women
making up about half of Aetna's management workforce

──────────── ◆ ────────────

Those women who want to dedicate themselves to being presidents
[can succeed], but I don't think women are as motivated to be
presidents of our companies.

U.S. real-estate mogul A. ALFRED TAUBMAN in 1990

I'm sorry my better half, Carolyne Roehm, couldn't be here today.
She could speak to you about something you would probably be more
interested in hearing about—fashion.

*investment banker HENRY KRAVIS in 1990, giving the
keynote speech at a luncheon sponsored by the Financial
Women's Association of New York*

──────── **C O U N T E R P O I N T** ────────

*Even more than the Pill, what has liberated women is that
they no longer need to depend on men economically.*

JANE BRYANT QUINN, columnist

──────────── ◆ ────────────

Like Plato, I find women to be more intelligent than men because they are more intuitive. But they often lack judgment. Therefore they use seduction at work. I am not against this. But they ought to use seduction in the service of the enterprise and not to prove that they are beautiful!

Quebec media magnate PIERRE PELADEAU *in 1990*

Duck feet? You're out. Pigeon toes? Out! Bowlegs, pimples, warts, moles, dark skin, scars, bad breath? Out! . . . [And] they must be virgins.

HAO YU-PING, *director of the flight attendant school at China Air, describing in 1992 the airline's demands in recruiting attendants*

──────────── C O U N T E R P O I N T ────────────

I'm not sure there's a lot that women can do about it. They're already working hard and are very qualified. It shouldn't be this way, but too many senior managers, and particularly CEOs, tend to want to pass their jobs along to someone who's the image and likeness of themselves.

JOHN H. BRYAN, CEO of Sara Lee Corp., a firm noted for its drive to promote women managers, on the slow progress of female advancement in America's corporate ranks

──────────── ◆ ────────────

Intelligent women tend not to be good-looking.

> KASET ROJANANIL, *Thai Air chief marshall, about*
> *complaints that his airline's flight attendants are not pretty*
> *enough, in the early 1990s*

─────────── **C O U N T E R P O I N T** ───────────

Beware of the man who praises women's liberation; he is
about to quit his job.

ERICA JONG

The labor shortage [in Japan] is so bad that we are actually having to use women for their brainpower instead of hiring them for their looks.

a recruiter for Japan's Asahi National Broadcasting Co., in 1992

[**W**e will] focus on phasing out female workers because they tend to quit sooner, usually after getting married.

Japan's Nomura Securities, the world's largest brokerage,
announcing in 1992 how it planned to phase out 2,000 jobs
over the next five years

──────────── **COUNTERPOINT** ────────────

I can't think of any other time that a women's issue has so affected politics. It has suddenly become clear that someone who does not respect women is not fit to be Prime Minister of Japan.

KII NAKAMURA, vice-president of the
Japan Housewives Association

─────────────── ◆ ───────────────

• 7 •

Science & Academe

Nature has determined a woman's destiny through beauty, charm and sweetness. Law and custom may have much more to give women that has been withheld from them, but the position of women will surely be what it is: in youth an adored darling and in mature years a loved wife.

SIGMUND FREUD in 1883

──────────── COUNTERPOINT ────────────

No man, not even a doctor, ever gives any other definition of what a nurse should be than this—"devoted and obedient." This definition would do just as well for a porter. It might even do for a horse. It would not do for a policeman.

FLORENCE NIGHTINGALE in 1859

When a woman becomes a scholar there is usually something wrong with her sexual organs.

FRIEDRICH NIETZSCHE *in 1888*

Direct thought is not an attribute of femininity. In this, woman is now centuries . . . behind men.

THOMAS ALVA EDISON *in* Good Housekeeping, *1912*

————————— COUNTERPOINT —————————

If I were asked . . . to what the singular prosperity and growing strength of that people [Americans] ought mainly to be attributed, I should reply: to the superiority of their women.

ALEXIS DE TOCQUEVILLE, *Democracy in America*

————————— ◆ —————————

The psychical consequences of penis-envy . . . are various and far-reaching. After a woman has become aware of the wound to her narcissism, she develops, like a scar, a sense of inferiority. When she has passed beyond her first attempt at explaining her lack of a penis as being a punishment personal to herself and has realized that that sexual character is a universal one, she begins to share the contempt felt by men for a sex which is the lesser in so important a respect.

SIGMUND FREUD *in 1925*

Character-traits which critics of every epoch have brought up against women—that they show less sense of justice than men, that they are less ready to submit to the great necessities of life, that they are more often influenced in their judgments by feelings of affection or hostility—all these would be amply accounted for by the modification in the formation of their superego which we have already inferred. We must not allow ourselves to be deflected from such conclusions by the denials of the feminists, who are anxious to force us to regard the two sexes as completely equal in position and worth.

SIGMUND FREUD *in 1925*

It would be preposterously naive to suggest that a B.A. can be made as attractive to girls as a marriage license.

Columbia University president GRAYSON KIRK *in 1967*

———————————— **COUNTERPOINT** ————————

Yes means yes, no means it's too small.

message on a sign made by women students in 1989 at Queen's University in Kingston, Ontario, who were annoyed by constant threats by male students of date rape, and whose slogan was "No means maybe, maybe means yes"

———————————— ◆ ————————————

When women are encouraged to be competitive, too many of them become disagreeable.

BENJAMIN SPOCK *in 1969*

Biologically and temperamentally, I believe, women were made to be concerned first and foremost with child care, husband care, and home care.

BENJAMIN SPOCK *in 1969*

─────────── C O U N T E R P O I N T ───────────

That the child is the supreme aim of woman is a statement having precisely the value of an advertising slogan.
　　　　SIMONE DE BEAUVOIR in 1952

───────────── ◆ ─────────────

Dreams, myths, and cults attest to the fact that the vagina has and retains (for both sexes) connotations of a devouring mouth and an eliminating sphincter, in addition to being a bleeding wound.

ERIK ERIKSON *in 1968*

─────────── C O U N T E R P O I N T ───────────

If they can put a man on the moon . . . why can't they put them all there?
　　　　graffiti, Kentish Town, U.K., circa 1986

───────────── ◆ ─────────────

There seem to be few women who manage to sustain elements of their femininity when public acclaim is part of their daily experience.

LORIENE CHASE, *clinical psychologist, in 1988*

Today's woman is a stressed-out, nervous person. She's competitive and doesn't like to yield to anything. She knows how to have an orgasm, but she isn't light, fun, or easy to be with.

U.S. psychologist TONI GRANT *in 1989*

That's another preconceived notion—that anything women invent is a household tool or a doll. But they also invented the bra, pink champagne and the ice-cream cone.

ETHLIE ANN VARE, *coauthor of the revisionist history* Mothers of Invention, *in 1989*

The things that make my life meaningful are: the taste of a good claret, the sound of a Beethoven quartet—a *late* Beethoven quartet—and the noise a woman makes as she approaches her third or fourth orgasm.

DR. R. P. CARROLL *on the Scottish BBC program* The Quest *in 1989*

─────────────── C O U N T E R P O I N T ───────────────

Femininity expresses the idea that there are things worth living for. Masculinity expresses the idea that there are things worth dying for.

JOHN WHEELER in *Touched with Fire*

─────────────────── ◆ ───────────────────

When Madonna grabs her crotch, the social order is effectively transgressed.

Florida State University professor CHIP WELLS *in 1991*

─────────────── C O U N T E R P O I N T ───────────────

I wouldn't want a penis. It would be like a third leg. It would seem like a contraption that would get in your way.

singer MADONNA in 1992

─────────────────── ◆ ───────────────────

There is a substantial and enlarging body of medical opinion that these deformities [small breasts] are really a disease.

excerpt from a 1992 memo from the American Society of Plastic and Reconstructive Surgeons to the U. S. Food and Drug Administration at a time when the dangers of cosmetic surgery on breasts caused the FDA to force the removal of silicone breast implants from the market

────────────── C O U N T E R P O I N T ──────────────

*A surgeon should have the eyes of a hawk, the heart of a lion,
and the hands of a woman.*

> CHRISTINA HILL, Canadian physician, in the
> early 1980s, quoting an axiom dating back to
> the 15th century

────────────────── ◆ ──────────────────

Some older men may say their erections aren't as big as they recall
them once being. But then their partner says, "Well, dear, you
overestimated them back then, too."

> DR. PAUL COSTA, JR., *a psychologist, speaking about male
> menopause in 1992 at the National Institute on Aging*

Women's studies is a jumble of vulgarians, bunglers, whiners, French
faddicts, apparatchiks, doughfaced party-liners, pie-in-the-sky
utopianists, and bullying, sanctimonious sermonizers.

> CAMILLE PAGLIA

◆8◆

Arts & Entertainment

Wommen are born to thraldom and penance
And to ben under mannes governance.
GEOFFREY CHAUCER, Canterbury Tales *(c. 1387)*

Nature has placed in the female body, in a secret and intestinal place, a certain animal or member which is not man, in which are endangered, frequently, certain humours, brackish, nitrous, voracious, acrid, mordant, shooting, and bitterly tickling.
FRANÇOIS RABELAIS *in* Gargantua and Pantegruel, *1533*

Very little wit is valued in a woman, as we are pleased with the few words of a parrot.
JONATHAN SWIFT, *English satirist and author (1667–1745)*

A dead wife under the table is the best goods in a man's house.
JONATHAN SWIFT *in* Polite Conversation, *1738*

Women have, in general, no love of any art; they have no proper knowledge of any; and they have no genius.

JEAN JACQUES ROUSSEAU *in 1758*

———————— COUNTERPOINT ————————

There is a woman at the beginning of all great things.
ALPHONSE DE LAMARTINE, 19th-century
French poet and statesman

———————— ◆ ————————

I am very fond of the company of ladies. I like their beauty, I like their delicacy, I like their vivacity, and I like their *silence*.

SAMUEL JOHNSON *in 1760*

Men are women's playthings; woman is the devil's.
VICTOR HUGO, *French author (1802–1885)*

When toward the Devil's house we tread,
Woman's a thousand steps ahead.

Mephistopheles in GOETHE'S Faust, *1808*

The generality of women appear to me as children whom I would rather give a sugar plum than my time.

JOHN KEATS *in 1818*

Man to command and woman to obey:
All else confusion.

> ALFRED, LORD TENNYSON *in 1847*

Regard the society of women as a necessary unpleasantness of social life, and avoid it as much as possible.

> LEO TOLSTOY *in 1847*

Woman is nature, hence detestable.

> CHARLES BAUDELAIRE *in* Les Fleurs du Mal, *1857*

Literature cannot be the business of a woman's life, and it ought not to be. The more she is engaged in her proper duties, the less leisure she will have for it, even as an accomplishment and recreation. To those duties you have not yet been called, and when you are you will be less eager for celebrity.

> ROBERT SOUTHEY, *advice to Charlotte Brontë*

Women should not be expected to write, or fight, or build, or compose scores; she does all by inspiring men to do all.

> RALPH WALDO EMERSON, *American writer*
> *(1803–1882)*

─────────── **C O U N T E R P O I N T** ───────────

As usual, there's a great woman behind every idiot.

> JOHN LENNON, English singer-songwriter
> *(1940–1980)*

◆

For men at most differ as Heaven and Earth,
But women, worst and best, as Heaven and Hell.
>   ALFRED, LORD TENNYSON, Idylls of the King, *1859*

There is not a war in the world, no, nor an injustice but you women
are answerable for it.
>   JOHN RUSKIN, Sesame and Lilies, *1865*

No woman can paint.
>   JOHN RUSKIN, *British critic and social theorist (1819–1900)*

I consider that women who are authors, lawyers, and politicians are
monsters.
>   PIERRE AUGUSTE RENOIR, *French painter (1841–1919)*

Time and circumstance, which enlarge the views of most men,
narrow the views of women almost invariably.
>   THOMAS HARDY, Jude the Obscure, *1895*

Clearly all disasters, or an enormous proportion of them, are due to
the dissoluteness of women.
>   LEO TOLSTOY *in 1900*

If men knew how women pass the time when they are alone, they'd
never marry.
>   O. HENRY *in 1905*

The way to handle wives, like the fellow says, is to catch 'em early, treat 'em rough, and tell 'em nothing!

SINCLAIR LEWIS *in* Main Street, *1920*

Women should be struck regularly, like gongs.

NOEL COWARD, Private Lives, *1930*

Women are like elephants to me: nice to look at, but I wouldn't want to own one.

W. C. FIELDS, *American comic actor* (1879–1946)

If you leave a woman, though, you probably ought to shoot her. It would save enough trouble in the end even if they hanged you.
ERNEST HEMINGWAY, *in a letter to his editor Maxwell Perkins, in 1943*

Men are infinitely more powerful and better painters than women. Women should be the power behind the throne.
artist HENRIETTE WYETH

. . . that unmentionable womb, that spongy pool, that time machine with a curse, dam for an ongoing river of blood.
NORMAN MAILER *in* The Prisoner of Sex, *1971*

The most important thing a woman can have—next to talent, of course—is her hairdresser.
JOAN CRAWFORD, *American actress (1904–1977)*

Women ought to be quiet. When people are talking, they ought to retire to the kitchen.
W. H. AUDEN *in* Table Talk, *1947*

I see—she's the original good time that was had by all.
BETTE DAVIS, *describing a starlet*

All women love semi-rape. They love to be taken. It was his sweet brutality against my bruised body that had made his act of love so piercingly wonderful. That and the coinciding of nerves completely relaxed after the removal of tension and danger, the warmth of gratitude, and a woman's natural feelings for her hero. I had no regrets and no shame . . . all my life I would be grateful to him, for everything. And I would remember him forever as my image of a man.

IAN FLEMING, The Spy Who Loved Me, 1963

If all the girls attending [the Yale prom] were laid end to end . . . I wouldn't be at all surprised.

DOROTHY PARKER

Boy meets girl; girl gets boy into pickle; boy gets pickle into girl.

JACK WOODFORD (1894–1971), on Hollywood film plots

What good are vitamins? Eat four lobsters, eat a pound of caviar—live! If you are in love with a beautiful blonde with an empty face and no brain at all, don't be afraid, marry her—live!

ARTUR RUBINSTEIN, Russian pianist and composer
(1887–1982)

A little bit of rape is good for man's soul.

NORMAN MAILER in 1972

You gotta marry a woman who's intelligent enough to be king while the king's out of town.

game-show host JOHN DAVIDSON

I don't like aging. The only thing you get is wisdom. How many guys are sexually attracted to someone who is fifty years old?

American rock singer GRACE SLICK

Once in a while, a man has to tell his wife to wash his socks— Simone [his late wife, Simone Signoret] liked it that way.

YVES MONTAND

Woman is made for man. Man is made for life.

Welsh-born actor RICHARD BURTON *in 1975*

I adore women. I am their total slave up to a certain point. I pamper them, cater to them, but when necessary, you have to bop 'em.

actor TELLY SAVALAS *in 1975*

You have to have a boy. If you don't have a boy, the name dies. And be sure to marry a lady who's young enough to have a baby.

FRANK SINATRA, *advice to son Frank Sinatra, Jr.*

I adore women as a whole. I enjoy them as a breed, like a dog. They're another species that you become endeared to. I don't mean that derogatorily, but in an admiring sense, like someone would appreciate a fine breed of horse.

author HENRY MILLER *in 1975*

American girls are like horses, very independent. They have never been controlled by anybody. But if you can break them in, they are very grateful, as all women are.

MICHAEL CAINE *in 1974*

--- C O U N T E R P O I N T ---

You know the problem with men? After the birth, we're irrelevant.

actor DUSTIN HOFFMAN

You know women—there's always something bothering them.
Welsh-born singer TOM JONES *in 1977*

Women are not equal and never could be.
American actor CHARLES BRONSON *in 1977*

The best players are men. . . . It is strange for me to see women players. I like the uniformity of one sex in the orchestra.
conductor ARTHUR FIEDLER *in 1978*

——————— **COUNTERPOINT** ———————

There's only one woman I know who could never be a symphony conductor, and that's the Venus de Milo.
MARGARET HILLIS, director of the
Chicago Symphony Orchestra

———————— ◆ ————————

What do women need money for?
rock singer MICK JAGGER *in 1978*

Brains are never a handicap to a girl if she hides them under a see-through blouse.
American singer BOBBY VINTON *in 1978*

When a woman says she wants to go out and get a job to express herself it usually means she's hopelessly behind in the ironing.
British actor OLIVER REED *in 1978*

Women love to be sat on and conquered. They love to be bossed.

Austrian actor MAXIMILIAN SCHELL *in 1978*

─────────────── **C O U N T E R P O I N T** ───────────

He smoked like Peter Lorre and drank like Humphrey Bogart and ate like Sydney Greenstreet and used up girls like Errol Flynn and then went out to a steam bath and came back looking like Clark Gable. It was all so reassuring that we never stopped to think that all these people are dead.

U.S. broadcaster HARRY REASONER
on film hero James Bond

───────────────── ◆ ─────────────────

Marriage is the best magician there is. In front of your eyes it can change an exciting, cute little dish into a boring dishwasher.

actor RYAN O'NEAL *in 1978*

Am I just cynical, or does anyone else think the only reason Warren Beatty decided to have a child is so he can meet babysitters?

talk-show host DAVID LETTERMAN *in 1991*

─────────────── **C O U N T E R P O I N T** ───────────

He's the type of man who will end up dying in his own arms.

MAMIE VAN DOREN, speaking of
sometime friend Warren Beatty

───────────────── ◆ ─────────────────

You gotta keep changing. Shirts, old ladies, whatever.
Canadian-born singer NEIL YOUNG

Marriage is very difficult. Very few of us are fortunate enough to marry multimillionaire girls with thirty-nine-inch busts who have undergone frontal lobotomies.
American actor TONY CURTIS *in 1980. In 1993, the 67-year-old actor married 30-year-old Lisa Deutsch, for his fourth marriage.*

Every woman loves the idea of a sheikh carrying her off on his white horse and raping her in his tent. It's a basic feminine instinct.
actor OMAR SHARIF *in 1981*

─────────── **C O U N T E R P O I N T** ───────────

Give a man a free hand and he'll run it all over you.
MAE WEST

──────────── ◆ ────────────

Marriage is a custom brought about by women who then proceed to live off men and destroy them, completely enveloping the man in a destructive cocoon or eating him away like a poisonous fungus on a tree.

Irish actor RICHARD HARRIS *in 1983*

In my view, a woman's sexuality cannot be separated from her whole personality. It's impossible to consider woman in isolation from man and the world we share. It seems to me that what happens in the vagina has more to do, in 1984, with H-Bombs than with G-spots.

D. M. THOMAS *in British* Cosmopolitan, *1984*

The only way to resolve a situation with a girl is to jump on her, and things will work out.

American actor LEE MARVIN *in 1984*

─────── C O U N T E R P O I N T ───────

A man has to be Joe McCarthy to be called ruthless. All a woman has to do is put you on hold.

MARLO THOMAS

───────── ◆ ─────────

Yeah, I hit her, but I didn't hit her more than the average guy beats his wife.

IKE TURNER *in 1985, on his stormy relationship with ex-wife Tina Turner*

Educating a woman is like pouring honey over a fine Swiss watch. It stops working.

author KURT VONNEGUT *in 1985*

You can't accept one individual's [opinion], particularly if it's a female and you know—God willing, I hope, for her sake it's not the case—but when they get a period, it's really difficult for them to function as normal human beings.

> JERRY LEWIS, *responding to a harsh review*
> *from a female Montreal* Gazette *critic in 1986*

The perfect woman has a brilliant brain, wants to make love until four in the morning—and then turns into a pizza.

> *rock singer* DAVID LEE ROTH *in 1988*

There are more men who are deeply interested in intellectual matters than women.

> NORMAN MAILER, *host of the 48th annual PEN*
> *International conference in New York in 1986, explaining the*
> *dearth of women panelists*

Ninety percent are undressed. The rest are swinging from chandeliers or something.

> *rock musician* GENE SIMMONS *in 1988 on his collection of*
> *about 2,000 Polaroid photos of groupies*

All a woman needs is vision, determination and a very rich husband who'll give her $112 million for a divorce.

> *caption for a 1988* EDWARD SOREL *caricature of* Lear's
> *magazine founder Frances Lear, former wife of TV producer*
> *Norman Lear*

My notion of a wife at forty is that a man should be able to change her, like a bank note, for two twenties.

actor WARREN BEATTY *in 1986*

It's a sad state of affairs when you can't make a murder mystery and kill anybody because you're going to offend a small group.

film director BRIAN DE PALMA *in 1990, on depicting murders of women in movies*

I believe that the husband should be the head of the household, that he should be the boss. . . . I know it's nonsense to believe that a woman doesn't have the same natural instincts and shouldn't have the same rights as a man, but that's the way I was brought up.

actor JAMES CAAN

─────────────── C O U N T E R P O I N T ───────────────

The male ego with few exceptions is elephantine to start with.
                                    BETTE DAVIS in 1962

───────────────── ◆ ─────────────────

Women can't stand that there is something more important than them. . . . Why can't they just be happy and like to raise kids and tip-toe through the daisies?

musician JOE WALSH *in 1988*

Sure, I like an independent woman . . . but not for my wife. Of course she should work . . . until it's time to take care of the kids.

actor ANTHONY DELON *in 1988*

I have an old-fashioned sense of a wife's obligations and always have been the malleable one in marital situations. I adapt myself one-hundred percent to my husband's life.

ELIZABETH TAYLOR *in 1988*

I still think there's some jobs women shouldn't do. I feel like woman was made to kind of be protected by the menfolk. That's what God meant for it to be. We're the weaker sex.

country singer KITTY WELLS *in 1988*

If you are covering local teas, you have got more women.

New York Times executive editor MAX FRANKEL in the late 1980s, explaining why the Times ran fewer front-page stories by and about women than other dailies. When the comment was published in The Washington Post, dozens of women Times employees reported for work with tea bags pinned to their garments

I knew I could strap a guitar around my neck and have girls lick my boot heels.

rock singer GENE SIMMONS in 1988, on why he chose a music career

I'll get married when I find a woman who greets me at the door the way my dogs do.

Golden Nugget Casino host GENE KILROY in 1988

I don't chase women. I just sit on my wallet and wait for them to come to me.

author MICKEY SPILLANE in 1988

[**W**omen] can be such a frightful, bloody nuisance. They are possessive, jealous, illogical, even when intelligent, and boringly domestic. And they will breed all the time.

novelist and TV writer SIMON RAVEN *in 1988*

Novels are like wives, you don't talk about them. But movies are different, they're like mistresses, and you can brag a bit.

NORMAN MAILER, *asked about the progress of his novel*
Harlot's Ghost *in 1988*

I play it down a lot, how strong I am. I don't go around being Miss Independent; I play it very sweet. Because whoever my boyfriend is, I want him to feel like a man.

actress CHARLOTTE LEWIS *in 1988*

I think every woman wants to look up to a man, if she has any sense.

KATHARINE HEPBURN *in 1988*

———————— C O U N T E R P O I N T ————————

*I don't need a man to rectify my existence. The most
profound relationship we'll ever have is the one with ourselves.*
actress SHIRLEY MACLAINE

———————————— ◆ ————————————

Dirty socks.

actor JOHNNY DEPP *in 1988,
citing a disadvantage of being a bachelor*

You have to be a little woman in his eyes. Today's woman competes with men, and a man doesn't want that.

actress ZSA ZSA GABOR *in 1988*

Women are great. When they dig you, there's nothing they won't do. That kind of loyalty is hard to find—unless you've got a good dog.

rock singer DAVID LEE ROTH *in 1989*

The vagina is really one part of the body we've actually been on both sides of. In one way we could look at it as a sort of homecoming.

author ERICH SEGAL's *husband-hero in* Doctors *(1989),*
before conducting his first pelvic examination

That was a faggy movie where all the women were men. Our movie depicts strong, bitchy women who don't just sit around. And no, I don't think they are too bitchy. Women can never be too bitchy.

actress ROSEANNE ARNOLD *in 1989 on the merits of her*
film She-Devil *versus* Steel Magnolias

Strong women leave big hickeys.

MADONNA *in 1989*

In love, I like men to dominate me as long as the affair lasts. To me, to be free means free to choose whose slave I want to be.

actress MELINA MERCOURI *in 1989*

I grew up believing that women should be nurturing and loving and let men take care of industry and science and all those complicated professions. I still believe that.

actress TERI COPLEY *in 1989*

I'll be dead before Bo really starts to age.

producer JOHN DEREK *in 1989, on the key to his successful marriage to actress Bo Derek, who is 30 years his junior*

Strong women disconcert me. The woman I found more appealing than any other was Marilyn Monroe. I never even met her, but it was quite obvious that she couldn't make it all alone, and this made me want to protect her, to possess this little blond cloud.

actor MARCELLO MASTROIANNI *in 1989*

I wish American women would go back to letting their husbands be the head of the family. I think American society was better off when women made being good wives and mothers their top priority. Nowadays, people are confused and uncertain about their roles in life.

Country singer BARBARA MANDRELL *in 1989*

Keeping that person must be your main priority—and that means he comes before your work.

BARBRA STREISAND *in 1989, on holding onto a boyfriend*

——————— C O U N T E R P O I N T ———————

Don't marry a man to reform him—that's what reform schools are for.

MAE WEST

◆

And as I'm trying to get her out the door, I realize that she's pretty cute. Then I realize I'm really hungry and I have nothing clean to wear and I have a wife right there in front of me. What the hell am I doing? "Unpack!" I told her.

DANNY BONADUCE, *former child-star in TV's* The Partridge Family, *describing a Japanese woman he married so she could obtain a green card, in 1989*

I feel like a real woman for the first time. You need to have a man to be fulfilled.

actress DELTA BURKE, *on her relationship with actor Gerald McRaney, in 1989*

I liked his arrogance, his vanity. Arrogance is a privilege of men of his calibre. Not so with women. Arrogant women are a plague.

MARLENE DIETRICH, *on Charlie Chaplin, in 1989*

I may have. She got in my face about a bunch of things going on. When a woman puts herself in the same position as a man, a woman needs something done to her.

country singer MICKEY GILLEY *in 1989, on accusations he struck former lover Connie Moore*

─────────── **C O U N T E R P O I N T** ───────────

I feel like I'm fighting a battle when I didn't start a war.
DOLLY PARTON

───────── ◆ ─────────

Sex and violence are one and the same.
rock musician PERRY FARRELL *in 1989*

Australia is still a male-chauvinist bastion and most of the women like it that way.
Australian actor PAUL HOGAN *in 1989*

I don't think having a naked woman strapped to a rack is sexist at all. And I don't think the fact that we pretend to slit her throat is violent. It's all show biz; it's entertainment. Can't everyone understand that?
BLACKIE LAWLESS, *member of the rock group W.A.S.P., in 1989*

─────────── **C O U N T E R P O I N T** ───────────

Sexiness is no longer defined just as whether [women] are desirable, but also as what [women] desire. The more liberated women become—economically, politically, and personally—the more erotic we are. Freedom is a lot sexier than dependency.

author NAOMI WOLF in 1992

───────── ◆ ─────────

When P.M.S. strikes around here, it's absolutely catastrophic, epidemic; it hobbles the whole organization.

> *TV talk-show host* GERALDO RIVERA, *in 1989*

The business has been taken over by low-life sluts.

> BETTE MIDLER *in 1990, on the rise of Roseanne Arnold and other female comedians*

───────── C O U N T E R P O I N T ─────────

All the scripts they send me are demeaning to women. If I can't play music in front of my four sisters, Mom, wife and daughters, I won't play it.

> *musician* CARLOS SANTANA *in 1992, on film scripts he has been asked to score*

───────────── ◆ ─────────────

It's a boy, just like I told her to have.

> *actor* ANDREW DICE CLAY *in 1990, on the birth of his son, Maxwell, to his companion Kathleen Monica*

Everybody got it wrong. I said I was into porn again, not born again.

> *rock star* BILLY IDOL *in 1990, denying rumors he had found God after being injured in a motorcycle accident*

We tried it as a cover. In light of the [Persian Gulf war], we thought a brunette was more appropriate.

> Vanity Fair *editor* TINA BROWN *in 1990, who put Cher on the cover rather than Marla Maples because, said Brown, brunettes present a stronger image*

COUNTERPOINT

The thing women have got to learn is that nobody gives you power. You just take it.

ROSEANNE ARNOLD

In 1965, we sat down one evening in a hotel and worked out that since the band had started two years earlier, I'd had 278 girls, Brian 130, Mick about 30, Keith six and Charles none.

> *Rolling Stones bassist* BILL WYMAN *in 1990, on the band's sexual exploits*

We've hung up bras from Montana in Wyoming and panties from South Dakota in Utah.

> *Aerosmith singer* STEVEN TYLER *in 1990, on the group's habit of hanging up fans' undergarments during concerts*

Jane will never be the six-thirty anchor. Not strong enough for the time period. Those are still male jobs, like morning-radio hosts.

> *talk-show host* LARRY KING *in 1990, forecasting the career of Jane Pauley*

I'd rather be hit by a gorgeous man than an ugly one.

actress ZSA ZSA GABOR *in 1990*

I've always maintained that there's a little bit of prostitute in all women. Or there should be. I think in order for a woman to be all that she hopes to be for a man, there has to be some of that there . . .

actress SHIRLEY JONES *in 1990*

The archetypes of women are the Madonna and the whore. We're all like that, but we repress one side or the other.

actress LAURA DERN *in 1990*

I sport a caveman mentality. A woman should be a lady on your arm and a whore behind your door.

musician NIKKI SIXX *of heavy-metal band Motley Crüe in 1990*

When you make them surrender to your power, that's sexy.

actor RAY SHARKEY *on what makes a woman sexy, in 1990*

I think women force men to be unfaithful. Men are unfaithful by nature occasionally, but not as constantly as I was.

actor ANTHONY QUINN *in 1990, on marital fidelity*

You shouldn't have to walk the streets in fear of being abused. You should get a man or a cab.

singer ROBERT PALMER *in 1990,*
asked to put himself in the place of a rape victim

All women, if they are really honest about it, would love to think they could get up onstage and have men sticking dollar bills in their panties.

actress KAY LENZ *in 1990*

The guy has to have control over his woman.

rap singer LL COOL J, *in 1990*

She is a sex goddess and, yes, she is my whore.

DAVID COVERDALE, *lead singer of the rock group*
Whitesnake, in 1990

Microphones are like mistresses. They can't answer back. You control them.

talk-show host LARRY KING

——————————— **COUNTERPOINT** ———————————

If I'm too strong for some people, that's their problem.
actress and British parliamentarian GLENDA JACKSON

——————————— ◆ ———————————

I rowed us to a secluded spot. . . . Right there, the estranged First Lady of Canada lent new meaning to the term "head of state."

GERALDO RIVERA *in 1991,*
on his alleged affair with Margaret Trudeau

Women dig [my act] because—I mean, you know this for a fact—women in private are much filthier than guys.

comedian ANDREW DICE CLAY *in 1990*

I'm not saying it didn't happen. But you'd think if it did, I would have remembered the first four or five hours.

singer WILLIE NELSON *in 1991, on a woman's claim that they had sex for nine straight hours, during which they performed a somersault*

Straight men need to be emasculated. I'm sorry. They all need to be slapped around. Women have been kept down for too long. Every straight guy should have a man's tongue in his mouth at least once.

MADONNA *in 1991*

I think they do, very probably.

rock star GEORGE MICHAEL *in 1991, when asked if his lovers try harder in bed because he's a celebrity*

——————————— COUNTERPOINT ———————————

Coming to terms with women as real people and not as fantasies is part of growing up.

rock star STING in 1988

————————————— ◆ —————————————

We do this because we want our guys to find us attractive.

actress JANE FONDA *in 1991, on why she exercises*

How can we have an invasion when the troops storm ashore and then change their minds?

comedian BOB HOPE *in 1991, on women in combat roles*

A woman should be home with the children, building that home and making sure there's a secure family atmosphere.

actor MEL GIBSON *in 1991*

The show was so real. A woman who follows her husband anywhere is a real woman.

actress EVA GABOR *in 1991, on the TV series* Green Acres

I once congratulated a woman friend on her daughter's recent success and she gave me a look like a lethal dart. But when a father sees his son succeed, there's an indescribable pride. It's the sense of continuity, the sense of immortality a father gets from his son.

actor MICHAEL DOUGLAS *in 1991*

The *truth* is that women aren't interesting before thirty. Men are kind of *born* people.

actress JODIE FOSTER *in 1991*

The only time I use them, they're either naked or dead.

movie producer JOEL SILVER *in 1991, on the women in his films*

——————— C O U N T E R P O I N T ———————

I have a lot of respect for women. My policy is I don't make fun of women or do gay jokes, dirty jokes, or cruel humor. There's so much hatred and malice in comedy today and that makes me very uncomfortable.

comedian and talk-show host JAY LENO in 1990

——————— ◆ ———————

Men may deny it, but I think their motivation to succeed, to be incredibly powerful and opulent and to maintain an overwhelming, titanic status in the community is for women. It is a sexual thing— it's done for either hands-on gratification or for the sexual allure. Power. That's what women are drawn to.

actor SYLVESTER STALLONE *in 1991*

I don't love women the way I love men. I love men pretty much. They're interesting. I'm more tolerant of them. I can say, "Oh, he's an asshole, but I love him." But if she's an asshole, she's an asshole.

actress DEBRA WINGER *in 1991*

"What about you and me and your daughter . . . ?"
"We're both too old for you."

exchange between WARREN BEATTY *and film producer*
JULIA PHILLIPS, *as reported by Phillips in her 1991*
autobiography

For me the highest level of sexual excitement is in a monogamous relationship.

WARREN BEATTY *to Norman Mailer in 1991*

My attitude is that if Picasso took a machine gun and cut down a line of grandmothers, okay, it would not affect my opinion of his art.

CAMILLE PAGLIA

What a looker that one is. I wonder how many guys she had to sleep
with before she got her BMW.

> actor JAMES WOODS, *remarking on the driver of a passing
> car during a 1992 interview*

It's amazing, the *Batman* promotion. . . . Have you seen the giant,
more than life-size, beautiful stand-up of Batman, sexy and [bulging].
More and more bulges now, genital bulges, are occuring. I mean, it is
very revolutionary, because it used to be Superman was always
absolutely neuter down there. You're starting to see the balls. I mean,
that's great. Now the look on his face under the mask is getting more
and more macho. He's sort of like the Marquis de Sade or something.

> CAMILLE PAGLIA *in* Vanity Fair *in 1992, on promotion
> materials for the release of the film* Batman

It ain't no big thing—I just threw her through the door.

> ANDRE YOUNG, *member of rap group N.W.A.,
> on the events leading up to a lawsuit against him in 1992*

So many times I have heard feminists ask why it is necessary for the
woman and not the man to stay at home with the children, and the
answer is one that seems obvious to me: a mother's breasts produce
the milk on which babies used to feed before infant formulas and
vanities took its place.

> actor MICHAEL CAINE *in his 1992 autobiography, complaining
> about Gloria Steinem's having placed him on what he described
> as "her list of international male chauvinist pigs"*

In relationships with women, I've found they lack understanding. The guitar understands everything. It doesn't talk back.
                guitarist NUNO BETTENCOURT *of the band Extreme, in 1992*

I'm not telling anybody, "If you're not happy, go out and screw around because your wife will become a dynamo for you," but I got to be honest with you, that's what happened to me.

country singer GARTH BROOKS *in 1992*

────────── C O U N T E R P O I N T ──────────

I don't think it will hurt my career if people know I'm married. I think it's much sexier to be in love with your wife.
actor PATRICK SWAYZE in 1989

──────────── ◆ ────────────

Women feel guilty about domination fantasies because they secretly want to be taken.

film director LIZZIE BORDEN *in 1992*

It's commonly known beautiful women work only on the basis of looks and not on gray matter.

actress TAWNY KITAEN, *in 1992*

If a guy cooks a gal dinner, he's going to be slept with, eventually.

actor JAY THOMAS *in 1992*

──────────── C O U N T E R P O I N T ────────────

*You're fooling yourself if you think you've got new and
improved males because you see three or four dudes out there
doing diapers and dishes.*

BILL COSBY

──────────────── ◆ ────────────────

I finally got it right.
                    actor JACK NICHOLSON *in 1992, on hearing of the birth of a
                    son after having had two daughters*

Why are you wearing this? I can't see your breasts.
                    film director OLIVER STONE *in 1992 to a female
                    Us magazine reporter*

──────────── C O U N T E R P O I N T ────────────

*Women have served all these centuries as looking-glasses
possessing the magic and delicious power of reflecting the
figure of man at twice its natural size.*

VIRGINIA WOOLF *in A Room of One's Own*

──────────────── ◆ ────────────────

If it makes Tina's nipples firm, then she goes with it.
                    Vanity Fair *writer* KEVIN SESSUMS *in 1992,
                    on how VF editor Tina Brown decides what makes a good story*

That woman suing him is a bitch. I don't care if he raped her. He should learn about himself and why he behaves like that. But equally, she should look at herself and look at the disgrace she is making of women.

singer SINEAD O'CONNOR *in 1992, on Desiree Washington's lawsuit against Mike Tyson, who was convicted of raping her*

·9·

The Sporting Life

Women's libbers are a pain in the ass. I treat women the way I always did, except I treat women's libbers different: if I catch one, I try and screw her a little harder.

daredevil EVEL KNIEVEL *in 1978*

There's nothing wrong with the ladies, God bless them; let them play. But what they're doing is eliminating much of the available time when young players can get on the course.

American golfer JACK NICKLAUS *in 1978*

People ask me how many children I have and I say one boy and seven mistakes.

boxer MUHAMMAD ALI *in 1985*

Ladies, here's a hint: if you're playing against a friend who has big boobs, bring her to the net and make her hit backhand volleys. That's the hardest shot for the well-endowed.

tennis star BILLY JEAN KING

─────────────── C O U N T E R P O I N T ───────────────

When I want to really blast one, I just loosen my girdle and let 'er fly.
> athlete BABE DIDRIKSON ZAHARIAS (1914–1956)

─────────────── ◆ ───────────────

Hit at the girl whenever possible.
> BILL TILDEN, *advice on playing mixed doubles*

Going to bed with a woman never hurt a ballplayer. It's staying up all night looking for them that does you in.
> *baseball manager* CASEY STENGEL

I bought 2,000 [video] tapes last week. I like action movies—Bronson, Eastwood, Reynolds, Schwarzenegger and Stallone. Bogart and Cagney. I'm not a guy to watch a lot of ladies crying.
> *baseball legend* WILLIE MAYS *in 1988*

Then I took her off her feet. I suaved her.
> *boxer* MIKE TYSON *in 1988, on his romance with actress*
> *Robin Givens*

Torture, pure hell, worse than anything I could imagine.
> ROBIN GIVENS *in 1988, describing her marriage to*
> *Mike Tyson*

One of these days they're going to make good wives, because that's all they do is clean.

> *high-school football coach* JOE BOB JOHNSON *in 1988 on the seven girls on the team's nine-member managing staff*

Physically fit, very attractive, and not too bright.

> *Chicago Bears tackle* PAUL BLAIR *in 1988, on the perfect woman*

No one will ever convince me that Ms. isn't short for mistake.

> *Canadian sports columnist* JIM TAYLOR *in 1988*

Men don't care about food—that's why it's so easy for them to go on a diet. But women *need* chocolate.

> *bodybuilder* CORINNA EVERSON *in 1988*

----------------- **COUNTERPOINT** -----------------

I'm not denyin' the women are foolish: God Almighty made 'em to match the men.

> GEORGE ELIOT (Mary Ann Evans)
> British writer (1819–1880)

----------------- ♦ -----------------

I have six grandkids—four girls, though.

> *Houston Astros coach* YOGI BERRA *in 1988*

It's like if you want to keep your husband, you lose twenty-five pounds and clean up your act.

>　　　*Florida sports promotion director* RON SAFFORD *in 1988,*
>　　　*on his state's effort to attract a major-league baseball team*

I don't like women who try to compete with men.

>　　　*free dive world-record holder* JACQUES MAYOL, *in 1988*

————————— C O U N T E R P O I N T —————————

Men love war because it allows them to look serious. Because it is the one thing that stops women laughing at them.

>　　　　　JOHN FOWLES, *The Magus*

————————————— ◆ —————————————

Girls should be like a good pitching staff. You've got to rotate 'em.

>　　　*retired L. A. Rams guard* DENNIS HARRAH *in 1988*

At some point these women were all normal little girls. Somewhere along the line they got sidetracked.

>　　　AL TRAUTWIG, *ABC announcer at the Calgary Olympics,*
>　　　*on the large number of women athletes participating*
>　　　*in the 1988 games*

If we wanted her to have a career, she wouldn't be having a child.

>　　　*hockey star* WAYNE GRETZKY *in 1989, denying that his move*
>　　　*to the L. A. Kings was prompted by wife Janet Jones's acting career*

─────────────── COUNTERPOINT ───────────────

A man's home may seem to be his castle on the outside; inside it is more often his nursery.

American writer CLARE BOOTHE LUCE
(1903–1987)

──────────────── ◆ ────────────────

Seeing the great skill and accuracy with which these guys fly is something. There are a few ladies, but if God meant for ladies to fly he would have made the sky pink.

U.S. hot-air balloonist NICK SAUM *in 1989*

I just don't think women should be umpires, period. I have three daughters and I'd hate for any of them to be out there listenin' to all the swearin' and stuff.

San Francisco Giants manager ROGER CRAIG *in 1989*

She plays like a man, and that means darn good.

poker champion THOMAS "AMARILLO SLIM" PRESTON
on poker champion Cyndy Violette, in 1989

A hamstring is like a sensitive girlfriend. If you push it, it's gone. You have to baby it. Give it lots of affection.

Olympic hurdler ROGER KINGDOM *in 1989*

I guess you would say I'm a male chauvinist. I don't disrespect women or anything, but I feel like if there's a disagreement, what the man says goes. I hate to see a weak man and a woman who walks all over him.

ERIC DICKERSON, *running back with the Indianapolis Colts, in 1989*

——————— **COUNTERPOINT** ———————

The American is hysterical about his manhood.
American novelist GORE VIDAL

————————— ◆ —————————

I'm pretty good for a girl.
actress PARK OVERALL *on her pool-playing skills, in 1989*

Women were created in a role of submission to men and should not be in a position of leadership.
BOB KNEPPER, *pitcher with the Houston Astros,*
on female umpires, in 1989

I made a good par at 18, so I won't go home and beat my wife.
golfer JACK NICKLAUS *in 1989*

The top eight women are excellent at their own standard, but the rest do little more than make up the numbers, and many of them are paid a lot of money for doing it. The men get very angry about that. They know very well that the crowds that come want to see men's tennis and not women's because our game is much more exciting and isn't over in thirty minutes.

tennis star STEFAN EDBERG *in 1989*

COUNTERPOINT

Seven men, thereabouts, are always there at it, it takes several to talk, several to look on and one or two to work, so whatever there is to do it always takes about the same number.

GERTRUDE STEIN

I should have kept her in foal constantly.

racehorse trainer D. WAYNE LUKAS *in 1989, on how he wishes his wife had more sons*

I don't know what kind of doctor I am. But watching all these beautiful sisters here . . . I'm debating whether I should be a gynecologist.

boxing champion MIKE TYSON *in 1989, after receiving an honorary degree from Central State University in Wilberforce, Ohio*

None of your business. I don't want to talk about it. I had my period.
> PAT CASH, *tennis player, in 1989 when asked about*
> *his disappointing performance at the Australian Open*

I told him to take a picture of his testicles so he'd have something to remember them by if he ever took another shot like the last one. For you ladies, that's t-e-s-t-i-c-l-e-s.
> *Indiana University basketball coach* BOBBY KNIGHT *in 1990*
> *when asked about a heated exchange he'd had with one of his*
> *players during a game*

Women by their nature are not exceptional chess players. They are not great fighters.
> *chess master* GARRY KASPAROV *in 1990*

I see the devil almost every day. When I look at a woman's eyes, I see the devil. When I look at a glass of liquor, I see the devil.
> MIKE TYSON *in 1990*

When I signed, I almost felt like I was getting married again—being tied down for five years.
> *baseball player* JOSE CANSECO, *on signing a $23.5-million*
> *deal with the Oakland Athletics in 1990*

Listening to a woman is almost as bad as losing to one. There are only three things that women are better at than men: cleaning, cooking, and having sex.
> *basketball star* CHARLES BARKLEY *in 1990*

I don't talk to people when I'm naked, especially women, unless they're on top of me or I'm on top of them.

> *pitcher* JACK MORRIS *in 1990, to a woman sportswriter who tried to interview him in the Detroit Tigers locker room*

It doesn't bother me. . . . We have never had total equality in women's athletics, and I don't know that we ever will have. . . . I guess there is women's mud wrestling.

> *Oklahoma Governor* HENRY BELLMON *in 1990, on the decision by the University of Oklahoma, later rescinded, to drop its women's basketball program*

The last few years they have had some dynamite-looking girls out there playing golf. And that's what the sport really needs . . . some striking female to take over and become the next superstar. It would have been Nancy Lopez, but Nancy turned to motherhood and so has her body.

> *CBS sports producer* FRANK CHIRKINIAN, *on why the Ladies Professional Golf Association hasn't grown in TV popularity, in 1990*

COUNTERPOINT

You come here to watch the game. You don't really need to see men sucking on women's parts, even if they're plastic.

> Boston baseball spectator JEANNINE ROBBINS in 1991, complaining about anatomically correct female blow-up dolls passed around the stands at Fenway Park

◆

I know I'm fertile; I've got the checkbook to prove it. But getting a couple of girls pregnant probably gave me a sense that there's no sweat: I can have kids anytime I want. It seems like anytime I've ever wanted something before, I've always been able to obtain it. Plus, I've had the security of knowing I'm a proven performer.

Kansas City Royals player GEORGE BRETT *in 1990,*
on the abortions obtained by two former girlfriends

Chess is a tough fight. A match can last hours, days, or weeks. It's tension. . . . Women can't concentrate for a long time.

world chess champion, GARRY KASPAROV,
in 1990, on women's ability to play chess

In a way [looks are a] part of ice-skating, which is an expression of grace and beauty. Besides, I think every man prefers looking at a good-looking woman and not at one shaped like a rubber ball.

ice-skater KATARINA WITT *in 1990*

——————— C O U N T E R P O I N T ———————

If a man watches three football games in a row, he should be declared legally dead.

ERMA BOMBECK

————————————— ◆ —————————————

I prefer girls who are young. When I eat a peach, I don't want it overripe. I want that peach when it's peaking.

former football player JIM BROWN *in 1990*

Women tennis players don't get as much money as the men because people come to see the men. I suppose it's the same with the film industry.

actor SEAN CONNERY *in 1990*

You don't tell me how to hit, and I won't tell you how to make babies.

New York Yankees second baseman STEVE SAX *in 1990,*
to a female art director who suggested he shift his bat
during a photo session

──────────── **C O U N T E R P O I N T** ────────────

What a gift—to give life, to bear a child. Strength comes from
that. Emotionally and spiritually, women may be able to lift
the world.

Buffalo Bills defensive lineman
BRUCE SMITH in 1991

──────────── ◆ ────────────

Yes, that's correct—20,000 different ladies. At my age that equals out to having sex with 1.2 women a day, every day since I was fifteen.

basketball star WILT CHAMBERLAIN *in 1991,*
on his claim to having slept with 20,000 women

We were happily married for eight months. Unfortunately, we were married for four and a half years.

golfer NICK FALDO *in 1991, on his ex-wife*

Let me tell you something about intelligence. You can get that from men. When I go into the bedroom with my woman, I don't want a bunch of educated crap.

football star JIM BROWN *in 1991*

──────────── COUNTERPOINT ────────────

Women's discontent increases in exact proportion to her development.

ELIZABETH CADY STANTON, American suffragette (1815–1902)

──────────── ◆ ────────────

If you can pick women, you can pick cattle. You look for good angularity, nice legs, and capacity.

hockey star BOBBY HULL *in 1991*

[Acting] is a very unmanly business. It's very much woman's work. . . . It's just a very lightweight business.

actor and boxer MICKEY ROURKE *in 1991*

They can wiggle their waggles in front of her face as far as I'm concerned.

VICTOR KIAM, *owner of the Remington shaver company of the New England Patriots, on harassment of a woman reporter by his players in 1991*

Girls don't belong in the water. Girls belong in the kitchen. When you see girls out in the water, you don't want to give them a wave because you know they can't surf. It's a rough sport and I can't handle seeing girls get hurt because they're like little precious items, you know, they're like little precious dolls. Girls can't take the pain, you know. When you have your babies and stuff, that's the most pain you can have.

professional surfer RICHIE COLLINS *in 1991*

―――――――――――― **C O U N T E R P O I N T** ――――――――

Tell them to go jump in the lake. Maybe they're not worth having around.

Olympic medalist speed-skater BONNIE BLAIR
in 1988, on boyfriends who pressure young
women not to become athletes

―――――――――――――――――― ◆ ――――――――――――――

I said that 80 percent of the top 100 [women tennis players] are fat pigs, but I overexaggerated a little bit. What I meant to say is that only 75 percent [are fat pigs].

tennis player RICHARD KRAJICEK *in 1992, on why female players don't deserve prize money equal to men*

[**T**hey] all start with a "K" because I struck out three times.

UCLA basketball coach GARY ADAMS *in 1992, on why his triplet daughters—Kimmy, Kristy and Kathy—have names starting with "K," the symbol for strikeout in baseball*

─────────────── C O U N T E R P O I N T ───────────────

I think it would help to deal with a lot of the challenges that young women face in their lives if they can stay involved in athletic activity.

BILL CLINTON in 1992 at a White House
ceremony to honor Lynette Woodard, the first
woman named to the Harlem Globetrotters
and Captain of the 1984 U.S. women's
basketball team

───────────────── ◆ ─────────────────

As long as those babes are lying out by the water with no tops on, I'll be at the pool.

U.S. basketball star CHARLES BARKLEY *in 1992, during a stopover in Monte Carlo enroute to the Barcelona Olympics as a member of the so-called "Dream Team"*

─────────────── C O U N T E R P O I N T ───────────────

The feminist movement had to happen. [Men] had to be awakened.

Chicago Bears linebacker MIKE SINGLETARY
in 1992

───────────────── ◆ ─────────────────

You confirmed it: women don't belong on a man's tennis court.

> JIM COURIER, *tennis star, complaining to a woman line judge at the U.S. Open in 1992*

They pushed me away like I wasn't there. My coach said, "You are like a girl."

> *Lithuanian Olympic basketball player* ARTURAS KARNISHOVAS *in 1992, after his team's defeat by the U.S. "Dream Team"*

· 10 ·

The Flame of Coexistence

Though you love your wife, do not tell her all you know; tell her some trifle, and conceal the rest.

HOMER *in the* Odyssey, *c. 800* B.C.

The vows that a woman makes to her lover
Are only fit to be written on air.

CATULLUS, *in* Carmina, *c. 60* B.C.

A woman who has lost her chastity will shrink from no other crime.

TACITUS *in* Annals, *c.* A.D. *100*

The wife . . . should lead a chaste life, devoted to her husband, and doing everything for his welfare. Women acting thus . . . generally keep their husbands devoted to them.

The Kamasutra of Vatsyayana, fourth century A.D.

Strife is the dowry of a wife.

OVID *in* Amores, *c.* A.D. *15*

Who does not tremble when he considers how to deal with a wife?

HENRY VIII *in 1521, writing in praise of marriage in a
paper entitled, "The Defence of the Seven Sacraments"—a
refutation of Martin Luther's challenge to Pope and Church.
Just six years later, Henry VIII initiated his first divorce,
from Catherine of Aragon*

Of women's unnatural, unsatiable lust, what country, what village
doth not complain?

ROBERT BURTON *in* The Anatomy of Melancholy, *1621*

—————————— **C O U N T E R P O I N T** ——————————

*The majority of husbands remind me of an orangutan trying
to play the violin.*

HONORÉ DE BALZAC

————————————— ◆ —————————————

Women have no moral sense; they rely for their behavior upon the
men they love.

JEAN DE LA BRUYÈRE *in 1688*

A woman will flirt with anybody in the world as long as other people
are looking on.

OSCAR WILDE

Sometimes I wonder if men and women really suit each other. Perhaps they should live next door and just visit now and then.

KATHARINE HEPBURN

The one charm of marriage is that it makes a life of deception absolutely necessary for both parties.

OSCAR WILDE

Men marry because they are tired; women, because they are curious. Both are disappointed.

OSCAR WILDE

——————— C O U N T E R P O I N T ———————

Ideally, couples need three lives: one for him, one for her, and one for them together.

English actress JACQUELINE BISSET

——————— ◆ ———————

The whole world is strewn with snares, traps, gins and pitfalls for the capture of men by women.

GEORGE BERNARD SHAW, Man and Superman, *1903*

——————— C O U N T E R P O I N T ———————

The trouble with some women is that they get all excited about nothing—and then marry him.

CHER

——————— ◆ ———————

On one issue at least men and women agree: they both distrust women.

H. L. MENCKEN

─────────────── **COUNTERPOINT** ───────────────

Women know about life and about how to get along with others, and are sensitive to beauty, and can yell louder. They know all about guys, having been exposed to guy life since forever, and guys know nothing about girls except that they want one desperately. Which gender is better equipped to manipulate the other?

GARRISON KEILLOR, host of the radio
program "Garrison Keillor's American Radio
Company," in *The New York Times* in 1992

────────────────── ◆ ──────────────────

A man may be a fool and not know it, but not if he is married.

H. L. MENCKEN

Madam, if I were your husband, I'd eat it.

WINSTON CHURCHILL, *in reply to a woman who
admonished him, saying, "If you were my husband I'd poison
your food."*

─────────────── **COUNTERPOINT** ───────────────

There aren't any hard women, only soft men.

actress RAQUEL WELCH

────────────────── ◆ ──────────────────

The most successful marriage is ever the one in which the wife believes the husband to be a compendium of all the refinements of wisdom and understanding, however an ass the husband may be.

author GEORGE JEAN NATHAN, *c. 1929*

A man likes his wife to be just clever enough to comprehend his cleverness, and just stupid enough to admire it.

playwright ISRAEL ZANGWILL

———————— C O U N T E R P O I N T ————————

Men are not given awards and promotions for bravery in intimacy.

writer GAIL SHEEHY

————————— ◆ —————————

Never go to bed mad. Stay up and fight.

comedienne PHYLLIS DILLER

Marrying a man is like buying something you've been admiring for a long time in a shop window. You may love it when you get it home, but it doesn't always go with everything else.

playwright JEAN KERR

──────── C O U N T E R P O I N T ────────

When he is late for dinner and I know he must be either having an affair or lying dead in the street, I always hope he's dead.

author JUDITH VIORST

If I ever marry it will be on a sudden impulse, as a man shoots himself.

H. L. MENCKEN

Beyond any doubt her sex is a mouth and a voracious mouth which devours the penis—a fact which can easily lead to the idea of castration. The amorous act is the castration of the man; but this is above all because sex is a hole.

JEAN-PAUL SARTRE *in* Being and Nothingness, *1943*

─────────── C O U N T E R P O I N T ───────────

Whenever you want to marry someone, go have lunch with his ex-wife.

actress SHELLEY WINTERS

──────────────── ◆ ────────────────

If love is the answer, could you please rephrase the question.

comedienne LILY TOMLIN

No man is regular in his attendance at the House of Commons until he is married.

British statesman BENJAMIN DISRAELI

─────────── C O U N T E R P O I N T ───────────

One good husband is worth two good wives; for the scarcer things are, the more they are valued.

BENJAMIN FRANKLIN

──────────────── ◆ ────────────────

It's impossible for a woman to be married to the same man for fifty years. After the first twenty-five, he's not the same man.

Farmer's Almanac *in* 1966

The better you treat a man and the more you show you love him, the quicker he gets tired of you.

ERNEST HEMINGWAY *in* To Have and Have Not

An archeologist is the best husband any woman can have: The older she gets, the more interested he is in her.

AGATHA CHRISTIE (1891–1976)

――――――――― **COUNTERPOINT** ―――――――――

Marriage makes you legally half a person, and what man wants to live with half a person?

GLORIA STEINEM

――――――――― ◆ ―――――――――

There's nothing in the world like the devotion of a married woman. It's a thing no married man knows anything about.

OSCAR WILDE

A girl must marry for love, and keep on marrying until she finds it.

actress ZSA ZSA GABOR

An exploding cigar which we willingly smoke.

cartoonist LINDA BARRY *on love*

─────── C O U N T E R P O I N T ───────

Oh, life is a glorious cycle of song, a medley of
extemporanea; and love is a thing that can never go wrong;
and I am Marie of Roumania.
                                DOROTHY PARKER (1893–1967)

───────────── ◆ ─────────────

My toughest fight was with my first wife.

                                                MUHAMMAD ALI

Being married is the best prison for a woman. It is a marvelous jail.
                                couturier PIERRE CARDIN *in 1979*

─────── C O U N T E R P O I N T ───────

I don't sit around thinking that I'd like to have another
husband; only another man would make me think that way.
                                actress LAUREN BACALL

───────────── ◆ ─────────────

Husbands are like fires. They go out if unattended.

                                                ZSA ZSA GABOR

─────── C O U N T E R P O I N T ───────

Outside every thin woman is a fat man trying to get in.
                        English journalist KATHARINE WHITEHORN

───────────── ◆ ─────────────

Santa is a sex symbol to some women. I've found over the years, especially for those who have a drink or two at parties and have tried—unsuccessfully in my case—to seduce old Santa.

> *Sixty-one-year-old* RALPH GERTZ *of Chicago, in 1990,*
> *on playing Santa for the previous 40 years*

One thing Nancy Reagan's hairdressers knew for sure is that she'd never have a "nooner" with anyone—she'd never mess up her hair in the middle of the day.

> *former Reagan hairdresser* ROBIN WEIR *in 1991, on*
> *revelations in Kitty Kelley's Reagan biography of an alleged*
> *affair between the First Lady and Frank Sinatra*

I turn my back for two and one-half hours on Thursday afternoon. I look up. She has him out the checkout counter, out the door, bagged and in her car. . . . I didn't even know what hit me.

> DIANE SAWYER *in 1991, on Kathie Lee Gifford, who*
> *eventually married Sawyer's erstwhile boyfriend Frank Gifford*

────────────── C O U N T E R P O I N T ──────────────

Sex used to be our most powerful weapon against men. Not any more. Not since they found out we like it. We lost a big one there. Women aren't faking orgasms anymore. They're hiding them. "I didn't feel anything. Oh, that? That was the hiccups."

American comedian DIANE NICHOLS in 1992

────────────── ◆ ──────────────

Andre Agassi is very, very intelligent, very, very sensitive, very evolved more than his linear years.

> BARBRA STREISAND, *on tennis star Agassi in 1992*

He was miserable [and] a man who said he was miserable was irresistible.

> GLORIA STEINEM *in 1992, on her short-lived romance with real estate and media mogul Mortimer Zuckerman. In early 1993 Zuckerman said he thought he could make a success of his newly acquired New York newspaper, the financially stricken* Daily News, *saying "Women prefer tabloids because their arms are shorter."*

───────── **C O U N T E R P O I N T** ─────────

When you're in love, you put up with things that, when you're out of love, you cite.

> writer JUDITH MARTIN (Miss Manners)

───────────── ◆ ─────────────

There's a big difference between being thirsty and being dehydrated.

> *Savannah, a character in* TERRY MCMILLAN's *1992 book* Waiting to Exhale, *on the virtues of holding out for the right man*

───────── **C O U N T E R P O I N T** ─────────

The average man is more interested in a woman who is interested in him than he is in a woman with beautiful legs.

> MARLENE DIETRICH (1901–1992)

───────────── ◆ ─────────────

Love is the pint of boiling water pouring into your stomach.

English actress EMMA THOMPSON *in 1992*

─────────────── **C O U N T E R P O I N T** ───────────────

The important thing in acting is to be able to laugh and cry.
If I have to cry, I think of my sex life. If I have to laugh, I
think of my sex life.

English actress GLENDA JACKSON

───────────────── ◆ ─────────────────

Why the courts don't tell a husband who has been living off his wife
to go out and get a job is beyond my comprehension.

JOAN LUNDEN, *host of* Good Morning America, *who earns a*
reported $2 million a year, in 1992 after being ordered to pay
her estranged husband $18,000 a month in maintenance costs

─────────────── **C O U N T E R P O I N T** ───────────────

Some of us are becoming the men we wanted to marry.

GLORIA STEINEM

───────────────── ◆ ─────────────────

He's not really my boyfriend. He's more like this thing I sit on . . .
when I can't find a chair.

comedienne JUDY TENUTA *in 1992*

Index to Quoted Subjects

Abbott, Diane, 96
Adams, Gary, 174
Adams, John, 85, 86
Addison, Joseph, 33
Agnew, Spiro, 91
Ali, Muhammad, 162, 185
American Society of Plastic and Reconstructive Surgeons, 125
Amiel, Barbara, 64, 65
Andrews, Hunter, 96
Anthony, Susan B., 86, 87
Antrim, Minna, 23
Appleton, Charles, 47
Aquinas, St. Thomas, 79, 80
Arden, Elizabeth, 112
Aristotle, 10, 17, 18, 19
Armani, Giorgio, 66
Armbrister, Kenneth, 98
Army Corps of Engineers, 54
Arnold, Roseanne, 145, 150
Ashai National Broadcasting Co., 119
Asquith, Herbert, 88
Astor, Nancy, 11, 62, 79
Auden, W. H., 132
Augustine, St., 78
Austen, Jane, 60
Austin, Mary Hunter, 62

Bacall, Lauren, 185
Bacon, Francis, 33

Bakker, Jim, 82
Bakker, Tammy Faye, 69
Balzac, Honoré de, 36, 37, 178
Barbi, Shane, 75
Barkley, Charles, 169, 175
Barry, Linda, 184
Barrymore, John, 40
Bates, Gordon, 91
Baudelaire, Charles Pierre, 26, 36, 129
Beatty, Warren, 141, 156
Beauvoir, Simone de, 75, 123
Beaverbrook, Lord, 41
Bellmon, Henry, 170
Berra, Yogi, 164
Bettencourt, Nuno, 158
Bierce, Ambrose, 29, 38
Bing, Stanley, 96
Bisset, Jacqueline, 179
Black, Danelle, 77
Black, Roy, 59
Blair, Bonnie, 174
Blair, Paul, 164
Bonaparte, Napoléon, 36
Book Marketing Council, U.K., 115
Bombeck, Erma, 171
Bonaduce, Danny, 147
Borden, Lizzie, 159
Brett, George, 171
Brokaw, Tom, 44
Bronson, Charles, 136

Brooks, Garth, 159
Brown, Byran, 55
Brown, Helen Gurley, 11, 64, 105
Brown, Heywood, 67
Brown, Jim, 171, 173
Brown, Tina, 150
Brown, Willie, 101
Bruce, Lenny, 41
Bryan, John, 117
Buchanan, Patrick, 30, 92, 107
Burke, Delta, 147
Burke, Edmund, 23
Burton, Richard, 134, 178
Bush, Barbara, 73, 110
Bush, George, 106
Butler, Nicholas Murray, 113
Butler, Samuel, 20

Caan, James, 141
Caine, Michael, 135, 157
Camus, Albert, 39
Canseco, Jose, 169
Capra, Frank, 40
Cardin, Pierre, 185
Carlson, Barbara, 104
Carmichael, Stokely, 41
Carpenter, Bill, 99
Carr, Barbara, 105
Carroll, R. P., 124
Cartland, Barbara, 68, 70
Casgrain, Therese, 22

Cash, Kellye, 66
Cash, Pat, 169
Catherine II, 93
Catullus, 177
Cavett, Dick, 41
Cayne, James, 115
Cervantes Saavedra, Miguel de, 36
Chamberlain, Lord, 90
Chamberlain, Wilt, 172
Chambers, Ernie, 104
Chanel, Coco, 27
Charles, Prince, 45
Charles XI, 33
Chase, Loriene, 124
Chaucer, Geoffrey, 127
Cher, 179
Cherry, Doug, 109
Chesterfield, Lord, 28, 34, 35
Chesterton, G. K., 29
Chirkinian, Frank, 170
Christie, Agatha, 184
Churchill, Winston, 180
Clark, Joe, 50
Clay, Andrew Dice, 149, 153
Cleveland, Grover, 87
Clinton, Bill, 13, 106, 110, 111, 175
Clinton, Hillary Rodham, 77, 106
Collins, Richie, 174
Compton, Ronald, 116
Confucius, 78
Connery, Sean, 172
Cool J, LL, 152
Copley, Teri, 146
Copps, Sheila, 114
Cornfeld, Bernie, 45
Cosby, Bill, 13, 160
Cosmopolitan magazine, 64

Costa, Paul, Jr., 126
Courier, Jim, 176
Coverdale, David, 152
Coward, Noel, 131
Cowley, Abraham, 21
Craig, Roger, 166
Crawford, Cindy, 72
Crawford, Joan, 132
Cresson, Edith, 65, 102
Crosbie, John, 95
Curtis, Tony, 138

Daoud, Alex, 99
Darwin, Charles, 27
Davidson, John, 134
Davis, Bette, 32, 132, 142
Davis, Reuben, 47
de Havilland, Olivia, 67
de Klerk, Marike, 72
Delon, Anthony, 142
Demosthenes, 19
Denton, Jeremiah, 92
De Palma, Brian, 141
Depp, Johnny, 144
Derek, John, 146
Dern, Laura, 151
Detremerie, Jean-Pierre, 105
Diamond, Roy, 46
Dickerson, Eric, 167
Dietrich, Marlene, 147, 187
Diller, Phyllis, 181
Dionne, Denys, 51
Dior, Christian, 55
Dirck, Joe, 101
Disraeli, Benjamin, 183
Donne, John, 20
Douglas, Michael, 155
Dryden, John, 21
Dumas, Alexandre, 39

Eastwood, Clint, 50
Edberg, Stefan, 168

Edison, Thomas, 10, 121
Edwards, Bob, 39
Eliot, George, 60, 164
Emerson, Ralph Waldo, 129
Ephron, Nora, 111
Erikson, Erik, 123
Esquire magazine, 42
Everson, Corinna, 164

Faldo, Nick, 172
Falwell, Jerry, 84
Fargo, James Congdell, 113
Farmer's Almanac, 184
Farrell, Perry, 148
Fenwick, Millicent, 92
Fetner, P. Jay, 52
Fiedler, Arthur, 136
Fields, W. C., 131
Fiorucci, Elio, 49
Fleming, Ian, 133
Flowers, Gennifer, 76, 109
Flynt, Larry, 42, 57
Foman, Robert, 114
Fonda, Jane, 12, 71, 154
Forgy, Larry, 103
Fortune magazine, 115
Foster, Jodie, 155
Fowles, John, 165
Frankel, Max, 143
Franklin, Benjamin, 33, 183
Frederick, Pauline, 114
French, Marilyn, 13, 74
Freud, Sigmund, 120, 121, 122
Friedan, Betty, 25, 102

Gabor, Eva, 112, 155
Gabor, Zsa Zsa, 63, 145, 151, 184, 185
Gadhafi, Muammar, 95, 96
Gagnon, Edouard Cardinal, 83

Garraway, Charles, 44
Gatling, Lafayette, 68
Gertz, Ralph, 186
Getz, Meir Yehuda, 83
Gibbons, Kaye, 10, 70
Gibson, Mel, 154
Gilley, Mickey, 147
Givens, Robin, 68, 163
Goethe, Johann Wolfgang
  von, 24, 128
Goldwater, Barry, 90, 98
Good Housekeeping
  magazine, 77
Goodman, Ellen, 93
GQ magazine, 56
graffiti: University of Texas,
  51; Kentish Town, U.K.,
  123
Grant, Toni, 124
Gratian, 20
Grechko, Georgy, 48
Gretzky, Wayne, 165
Grove, Frederick Philip, 38
Gunter, Carl, 99

Hardy, Thomas, 130
Harding, Warren, 89
Harrah, Dennis, 165
Harrelson, Woody, 52
Harris, Richard, 138
Hartley, Fred, 114
Hatfield, Mark, 91
Hebrew saying, 79
Heflin, Howell, 100
Hegel, Georg, 24, 87
Heine, Heinrich, 36
Heiss, Carol, 75
Helmsley, Leona, 115
Hemingway, Ernest, 132,
  184
Henry VIII, 178
Henry, O., 130

Hepburn, Katharine, 36,
  144, 179
Herodotus, 17
Higuchi, Keiko, 58
Hill, Christina, 126
Hillis, Margaret, 136
Hinckley, Gordon, 84
Hoffman, Abbie, 11, 41
Hoffman, Dustin, 135
Hogan, Paul, 148
Holmes, Oliver Wendell, 38
Homer, 177
Hope, Bob, 154
Howland, Joy, 76
Hubbard, Kin, 41
Hugo, Victor, 128
Hull, Bobby, 173
Humphrey, Gordon, 95

Idol, Billy, 149
Ishihara, Shintaro, 102

Jackman, Nancy, 82
Jackson, Glenda, 152, 188
Jagger, Mick, 103, 136
James, Walter, 48
Jefferson, Thomas, 85
John of Salisbury, 79
John Paul II (pope), 82
Johnson, Don, 54
Johnson, Joe Bob, 164
Johnson, Samuel, 5, 34, 128
joke, feminist, 10, 51
Jones, Ben, 94
Jones, Shirley, 151
Jones, Tom, 136
Jong, Erica, 40, 118
Jung, Carl, 29
Juvenal, 19, 31

Kabler, James, III, 113
Kamasutra, 177

Kant, Immanuel, 22, 35
Karnishovas, Arturas, 176
Kasparov, Garry, 169, 171
Keats, John, 24, 128
Keillor, Garrison, 42, 180
Keith, David, 50
Kellet, Caroline, 66
Kempton, Sally, 65
Kennedy, Ted, 100
Kerr, Jean, 181
Khamenei, Ayatollah, 82
Kiam, Victor, 173
Kilroy, Gene, 143
Kimball, Spencer, 83
King, Billie Jean, 162
King, Larry, 150, 152
Kingdom, Roger, 166
Kinder, Doris, 48
Kinison, Sam, 48
Kipling, Rudyard, 38
Kirk, Grayson, 122
Kitaen, Tawny, 159
Klein, Calvin, 38
Knepper, Bob, 167
Knievel, Evel, 162
Knight, Bobby, 169
Knox, John, 81, 85
Konnyu, Ernest, 97
Krajicek, Richard, 174
Krantz, Judith, 76
Kravis, Henry, 116
Kubrick, Stanley, 59
Kukrety, Prem, 51

La Bruyère, Jean de, 178
Ladeira, Luiz, 55
Laing, R. D., 22
Lamartine, Alphonse de,
  128
Lamb, William, 24
Landers, Ann, 67
Lawless, Blackie, 148

Leacock, Stephen, 112
Leary, Timothy, 26
Lefebvre, Yvon, 45
Lennon, John, 129
Leno, Jay, 155
Lenz, Kay, 152
Letterman, David, 137
Lewis, Charlotte, 144
Lewis, Jerry, 140
Lewis, Sinclair, 131
Limbaugh, Rush, 53, 55
Lincoln, Abraham, 25
Locke, John, 21
Lombard, Carole, 62
Loos, Anita, 61, 63
Loyola, St. Ignatius, 81
Luce, Clare Boothe, 11, 62, 166
Lukas, D. Wayne, 168
Lukens, Buz, 102
Lunden, Joan, 188
Luther, Martin, 10, 20, 80

Mackey, Isabella, 69
MacLaine, Shirley, 144
Madonna, 113, 125, 145, 154
Mailer, Norman, 132, 133, 140, 144
Mandrell, Barbara, 146
Mannes, Marya, 71
Marcos, Ferdinand, 95
Marcuse, Phil, 108
Marks, Jerome, 51
Marsden, Michael, 47
Martin, Judith, 187
Marvin, Lee, 139
Marx, Groucho, 40
Mastroianni, Marcello, 146
Maxwell, Robert, 46
Mayol, Jacques, 165
Mays, Willie, 163
McClung, Nellie, 73, 89

McCoy, Billy, 53
McGinley, Phyllis, 35
McLaughlin, Audrey, 94, 98
McMillan, Terry, 187
Mead, Margaret, 30
Meir, Golda, 45, 83, 103
Menander, 12
Mencken, H. L., 29, 180, 182
Menkes, Suzy, 53
Mercouri, Melina, 145
Meshel, Robert, 46
Mestrinho, Gilberto, 100
Michael, George, 154
Midler, Bette, 149
Miller, Henry, 134
Milton, John, 33
Mojadedi, Sibjhatullah, 105
Montand, Yves, 40, 134
More, Thomas, 32
Morris, Jack, 170

Nachman, Jerry, 52
Nakamura, Kii, 119
Nash, Ogden, 39
Nathan, George Jean, 181
Nelson, Willie, 153
Neuharth, Allen, 42
Newsweek magazine, 30
New York Herald, 26
New York Times, 64, 88
Nichols, Diane, 186
Nicholson, Jack, 160
Nicklaus, Jack, 162, 167
Nietzsche, Friedrich, 27, 28, 34, 121
Nightingale, Florence, 120
Nin, Anaïs, 71
Nixon, Patricia, 103
Nixon, Richard, 103
Nomura Securities, 119

O'Connor, Sandra Day, 52
O'Connor, Sinead, 161
O'Neal, Ryan, 137
Orbach, Florence, 102
O'Rourke, P. J., 43, 50
Overall, Park, 167
Ovid, 31, 178

Paglia, Camille, 11, 71, 72, 77, 126, 156, 157
Palmer, Robert, 151
Parker, Dorothy, 63, 133, 185
Parton, Dolly, 148
Pearson, Judy, 108
Pearson, Maryon, 20
Peck, Jon, 95
Peladeau, Pierre, 117
Pendleton, Don, 42
Perot, Ross, 106, 107
Perriam, Wendy, 83
Phillips, Julia, 156
Pius XI (pope), 81
Plato, 17
Plutarch, 9, 31, 32
Poncy, Charles, 93
Pope, Alexander, 22, 24
Preston, Thomas, 166
Pythagoras, 17

Quayle, Dan, 97, 99, 101
Quayle, Marilyn, 74, 91
Queen's University, 122
Quinn, Anthony, 151
Quinn, Jane Bryant, 116

Rabelais, François, 127
Rather, Dan, 54
Raven, Simon, 144
Reagan, Ronald, 40, 92, 93
Reasoner, Harry, 137
Reddy, Helen, 44

Redgrave, Lynn, 73
Reed, Oliver, 136
Renfro, Anthony, 46
Renoir, Pierre Auguste, 10, 130
Richelieu, Cardinal, 81
Richter, Geraldine, 70
Ritter, Erika, 21
Rivera, Geraldo, 149, 152
Rivers, Joan, 94
Robbins, Jeannine, 170
Robertson, Pat, 56, 82
Robinson-Rice, Muriel, 73
Rojananil, Kaset, 118
Romanoff, Nicholas, 54
Rooney, Andy, 52, 57
Roosevelt, Eleanor, 18
Roosevelt, Theodore, 88, 89
Rosenthal, A. M., 72
Roth, David Lee, 140, 145
Rourke, Mickey, 173
Rousseau, Jean-Jacques, 23, 34, 35, 128
Rubinstein, Artur, 133
Ruskin, John, 130
Russell, Jane, 67

Sabia, Laura, 47
Sadoff, Melissa, 66
Safford, Ron, 165
Santana, Carlos, 149
Sargent, Claire, 109
Sartre, Jean-Paul, 183
Saum, Nick, 166
Savage, Gus, 98
Savalas, Telly, 134
Savant, Marilyn Vos, 63
Sawyer, Diane, 186
Sax, Steve, 172
Schell, Maximilian, 137
Schiffren, Lisa, 108

Schlafly, Phyllis, 11, 67, 70, 75
Schopenhauer, Arthur, 25, 26
Segal, Erich, 145
Sellman, Jane, 74
Sessums, Kevin, 160
Shakespeare, William, 21, 32
Sharif, Omar, 138
Sharkey, Ray, 151
Shaw, George Bernard, 39, 89, 179
Sheehy, Gail, 181
Silver, Joel, 155
Simmons, Gene, 140, 143
Simms, Steve, 94
Simpson, Alan, 108
Simpson, Wallis Warfield, 61
Sinatra, Frank, 110, 134
Singletary, Mike, 175
Sixx, Nikki, 151
Slick, Grace, 134
Smith, Bruce, 172
Smith, Liz, 66
Socrates, 31
Soffer, Don, 44
Sorel, Edward, 140
Southey, Robert, 129
Spencer, Earl of, 48
Spiceland, Flip, 50
Spillane, Mickey, 143
Spock, Benjamin, 10, 123
Stafford, Jean, 28
Staller, Ilona, 101
Stallone, Sylvester, 156
Stanton, Elizabeth Cady, 86, 173
Steichen, Edward, 19
Stein, Gertrude, 19, 168

Steinem, Gloria, 30, 45, 62, 67, 184, 187, 188
Stendhal, 24
Stengel, Casey, 163
Sting, 154
Stone, Oliver, 160
Stone, Roger, 101
Streisand, Barbra, 74, 146, 187
Swayze, Patrick, 159
Swift, Jonathan, 127

Tacitus, 177
Tailhook Convention, 53
Talmud, 80
Taubman, Alfred, 116
Taylor, Elizabeth, 142
Taylor, Jim, 164
Teitelbaum, Hubert, 47
Tennyson, Alfred, Lord, 26, 37, 129, 130
Tenuta, Judy, 188
Terry, Randall, 46, 58
Thatcher, Denis, 104
Thatcher, Margaret, 29, 69, 95, 97
Thomas, D. M., 139
Thomas, Jay, 159
Thomas, Marlo, 68, 139
Thompson, Emma, 188
Thurber, James, 41
Tilden, Bill, 163
Tocqueville, Alexis de, 121
Tolstoy, Leo, 10, 28, 129, 130
Tomlin, Lily, 5, 183
Trautwig, Al, 165
Trudeau, Margaret, 98
Trump, Donald, 9, 49, 50, 51
Truth, Sojourner, 69, 80
Tucker, Sophie, 61
Turner, Lana, 63

Turner, Ted, 12, 43, 44, 46
Turner, Ike, 139
Tyler, Stephen, 150
Tyrrell, R. Emmett, Jr., 58
Tyson, Mike, 163, 168, 169

University of Texas graffiti,
    See graffiti: University of
    Texas.

Van Buren, Abigail, 70
Vander Zalm, William, 97
Van Doren, Mamie, 61,
    137
Vare, Ethlie Ann, 124
Vernon, Robert, 58
Victoria, Queen, 60
Vidal, Gore, 167
Vinton, Bobby, 136
Viorst, Judith, 182
Vonnegut, Kurt, 139

Walesa, Lech, 91
Walsh, Joe, 142
Wayne, Lois, 81
Weir, Robin, 96, 186
Welch, Racquel, 180
Wells, Chip, 125
Wells, Kitty, 142
Werner, A. Mat, 56
West, Mae, 61, 138, 147
West, Rebecca, 69
Wexner, Leslie, 113
Wheeler, John, 125
White, Byron, 52
White, Vanna, 71
Whitehorn, Katharine, 185
Whitton, Charlotte, 100
Whistler, James McNeill, 100
Wilde, Oscar, 27, 38, 39,
    178, 179, 184
Williams, Clayton, 99
Wilson, Chris, 104

Winger, Debra, 75, 156
Winters, Shelley, 183
Witt, Katarina, 171
Wolf, Naomi, 148
Woodford, Jack, 133
Woods, James, 47, 157
Woolf, Virginia, 9, 88,
    160
Wordsworth, William, 33
Wyeth, Henriette, 132
Wyman, Bill, 150
Wynette, Tammy, 76

Yatch, Larry, 109
Yeltsin, Boris, 106
Young, Andre, 157
Young, Neil, 138
Yu-Ping, Hao, 117

Zaharias, Babe, 163
Zangwill, Israel, 181